Nestlé®

COLLECTION

Publications International, Ltd.

Favorite Brand Name Recipes at www.fbnr.com

Photography: Stephen Hamilton Photographics, Inc.
Photographers: Stephen Hamilton, Tate Hunt
Photographers' Assistant: Tom Gajda
Prop Stylists: Paula Walters, Tom Hamilton
Food Stylists: Chris Ingegno, Susie Skoog
Assistant Food Stylists: Sara Cruz, Carol Radford

Pictured on the front cover *(clockwise from top left):* Original Nestlé® Toll House® Chocolate Chip Cookies *(page 4),* Nestlé® Toll House® Chocolate Chip Pie *(page 68),* Layers of Love Chocolate Brownies *(page 42)* and Chocolate Rhapsody *(page 160).*

Pictured on the back cover: Chocolate Truffle Tart *(page 82).*

ISBN: 0-7853-8263-1

Library of Congress Control Number: 2002114630

Manufactured in China.

8 7 6 5 4 3 2 1

Microwave Cooking: Microwave ovens vary in wattage. Use the cooking times as guidelines and check for doneness before adding more time.

Contents

Favorite Cookies

Original Nestlé® Toll House® Chocolate Chip Cookies

2¼ cups all-purpose flour
1 teaspoon baking soda
1 teaspoon salt
1 cup (2 sticks) butter or margarine, softened
¾ cup granulated sugar
¾ cup packed brown sugar
1 teaspoon vanilla extract
2 large eggs
2 cups (12-ounce package) NESTLÉ TOLL HOUSE
    Semi-Sweet Chocolate Morsels
1 cup chopped nuts

PREHEAT oven to 375°F.

COMBINE flour, baking soda and salt in small bowl. Beat butter, granulated sugar, brown sugar and vanilla extract in large mixer bowl until creamy. Add eggs, one at a time, beating well after each addition. Gradually beat in flour mixture. Stir in morsels and nuts. Drop by rounded tablespoon onto ungreased baking sheets.

BAKE for 9 to 11 minutes or until golden brown. Cool on baking sheets for 2 minutes; remove to wire racks to cool completely.

Makes about 5 dozen cookies

Pan Cookie Variation
GREASE 15 × 10-inch jelly-roll pan. Prepare dough as above. Spread into prepared pan. Bake for 20 to 25 minutes or until golden brown. Cool in pan on wire rack. Makes 4 dozen bars.

Island Cookies

1⅔ cups all-purpose flour
¾ teaspoon baking powder
½ teaspoon baking soda
½ teaspoon salt
¾ cup (1½ sticks) butter, softened
¾ cup packed brown sugar
⅓ cup granulated sugar
1 teaspoon vanilla extract
1 large egg
1¾ cups (11.5-ounce package) NESTLÉ TOLL HOUSE Milk Chocolate Morsels
1 cup flaked coconut, toasted, if desired
1 cup chopped walnuts

PREHEAT oven to 375°F.

COMBINE flour, baking powder, baking soda and salt in small bowl. Beat butter, brown sugar, granulated sugar and vanilla extract in large mixer bowl until creamy. Beat in egg. Gradually beat in flour mixture. Stir in morsels, coconut and nuts. Drop by slightly rounded tablespoon onto ungreased baking sheets.

BAKE for 8 to 11 minutes or until edges are lightly browned. Cool on baking sheets for 2 minutes; remove to wire racks to cool completely.

Makes about 3 dozen cookies

Note: NESTLÉ TOLL HOUSE Semi-Sweet Chocolate Morsels, Semi-Sweet Chocolate Mini Morsels, Premier White Morsels or Butterscotch Flavored Morsels may be substituted for the Milk Chocolate Morsels.

Molasses Spice Cookies

1¾ cups all-purpose flour
1 teaspoon baking soda
1 teaspoon ground ginger
1 teaspoon ground cinnamon
¼ teaspoon ground cloves
¼ teaspoon salt
1 cup granulated sugar
¾ cup (1½ sticks) butter or margarine, softened
1 large egg
¼ cup unsulphured molasses
2 cups (12-ounce package) NESTLÉ TOLL HOUSE Premier White Morsels
1 cup finely chopped walnuts

COMBINE flour, baking soda, ginger, cinnamon, cloves and salt in small bowl. Beat sugar and butter in large mixer bowl until creamy. Beat in egg and molasses. Gradually beat in flour mixture. Stir in morsels. Refrigerate for 20 minutes or until slightly firm.

PREHEAT oven to 375°F.

ROLL dough into 1-inch balls; roll in walnuts. Place on ungreased baking sheets.

BAKE for 9 to 11 minutes or until golden brown. Cool on baking sheets for 2 minutes; remove to wire racks to cool completely. *Makes about 2½ dozen cookies*

tip

To soften butter for use in batters and doughs, place 1 stick of butter on a microwave-safe plate and heat at LOW (30%) power about 30 seconds or just until softened.

Double Chocolate Peanut Butter Thumbprint Cookies

1½ cups all-purpose flour
⅓ cup NESTLÉ TOLL HOUSE Baking Cocoa
1½ teaspoons baking powder
¼ teaspoon salt
2 cups (12-ounce package) NESTLÉ TOLL HOUSE Semi-Sweet Chocolate
    Morsels, *divided*
1 cup granulated sugar
    About 1 cup chunky or smooth peanut butter (not all-natural), *divided*
⅓ cup butter or margarine, softened
1½ teaspoons vanilla extract
2 large eggs

PREHEAT oven to 350°F.

COMBINE flour, cocoa, baking powder and salt in small bowl. Melt *1 cup* morsels in small, *heavy-duty* saucepan over low heat; stir until smooth. Beat sugar, *⅓ cup* peanut butter, butter and vanilla extract in large mixer bowl until creamy. Beat in melted chocolate. Add eggs, one at a time, beating well after each addition. Gradually beat in cocoa mixture. Stir in *remaining* morsels. Cover; refrigerate just until firm.

SHAPE into 1½-inch balls. Place 2 inches apart on ungreased baking sheets. Press thumb into tops to make about ½-inch-deep depressions. Fill each depression with about ½ teaspoon peanut butter.

BAKE for 10 to 15 minutes or until sides are set but centers are still slightly soft. Cool on baking sheets for 2 minutes; remove to wire racks to cool completely.

Makes 3½ dozen cookies

Chocolate Chip Shells

2 cups all-purpose flour

1⅓ cups (about 8 ounces) NESTLÉ TOLL HOUSE Semi-Sweet Chocolate Morsels, *divided*

4 large eggs

1 cup granulated sugar

1 tablespoon orange liqueur (such as Cointreau) or 1 teaspoon orange extract

1 teaspoon vanilla extract

2 tablespoons (about 1 orange) grated orange peel

1 cup (2 sticks) unsalted butter, melted

Sifted powdered sugar

PREHEAT oven to 350°F. Generously grease and flour madeleine baking pan(s).

COMBINE flour and *1 cup* morsels in medium bowl. Beat eggs, granulated sugar, orange liqueur, vanilla extract and orange peel in large mixer bowl until light in color. Fold flour mixture and butter alternately into egg mixture, beginning and ending with flour mixture. Spoon heaping tablespoon of batter into each prepared mold.

BAKE for 10 to 12 minutes or until wooden pick inserted in center comes out clean. Cool in pan(s) for 1 minute. With tip of knife, release onto wire racks to cool completely. Wash, grease and flour pan(s). Repeat with *remaining* batter.

SPRINKLE madeleines very lightly with powdered sugar. Microwave *remaining* morsels in *heavy-duty* resealable plastic food storage bag on HIGH (100%) power for 30 seconds; knead bag to mix. Microwave at additional 10-second intervals, kneading until smooth. Cut a small hole in corner of bag; squeeze to drizzle over madeleines. Allow chocolate to cool and set before serving.   *Makes about 2½ dozen madeleines*

Chunky Milk Chocolate Chip Cookies

   2 cups all-purpose flour
   1 teaspoon baking soda
   ¼ teaspoon salt
1¼ cups packed brown sugar
   1 cup (2 sticks) butter or margarine, softened
   1 teaspoon vanilla extract
   1 large egg
1¾ cups (11.5-ounce package) NESTLÉ TOLL HOUSE Milk Chocolate Morsels
   1 cup chopped nuts
   1 cup raisins

PREHEAT oven to 375°F.

COMBINE flour, baking soda and salt in small bowl. Beat sugar, butter and vanilla extract in large mixer bowl until creamy. Beat in egg. Gradually beat in flour mixture. Stir in morsels, nuts and raisins. Drop by heaping tablespoon onto ungreased baking sheets; flatten slightly.

BAKE for 9 to 11 minutes or until edges are lightly browned. Cool on baking sheets for 2 minutes; remove to wire racks to cool completely.   *Makes 2½ dozen cookies*

Double Chocolate Dream Cookies

2¼ cups all-purpose flour
   ½ cup NESTLÉ TOLL HOUSE Baking Cocoa
   1 teaspoon baking soda
   ½ teaspoon salt
   1 cup (2 sticks) butter or margarine, softened
   1 cup packed brown sugar
   ¾ cup granulated sugar
   1 teaspoon vanilla extract
   2 large eggs
   2 cups (12-ounce package) NESTLÉ TOLL HOUSE Semi-Sweet Chocolate
      Morsels

PREHEAT oven to 375°F.

COMBINE flour, cocoa, baking soda and salt in small bowl. Beat butter, brown sugar, granulated sugar and vanilla extract in large mixer bowl until creamy. Beat in eggs for about 2 minutes or until light and fluffy. Gradually beat in flour mixture. Stir in morsels. Drop by rounded tablespoon onto ungreased baking sheets.

BAKE for 8 to 10 minutes or until cookies are puffed. Cool on baking sheets for 2 minutes; remove to wire racks to cool completely.   *Makes about 4½ dozen cookies*

Butterscotch Thins

2⅔ cups all-purpose flour

1½ teaspoons baking soda

1⅔ cups (11-ounce package) NESTLÉ TOLL HOUSE Butterscotch Flavored Morsels

1 cup (2 sticks) butter or margarine, cut into pieces

1⅓ cups packed brown sugar

2 large eggs

1½ teaspoons vanilla extract

⅔ cup finely chopped nuts

PREHEAT oven to 375°F.

COMBINE flour and baking soda in medium bowl.

MICROWAVE morsels and butter in large, microwave-safe mixer bowl on MEDIUM-HIGH (70%) power for 1 minute; stir. Microwave at additional 10- to 20-second intervals, stirring until smooth. Beat in sugar, eggs and vanilla extract. Gradually beat in flour mixture; stir in nuts. Cover; refrigerate for about 1 hour or until firm. Shape into two 14 × 1½-inch logs; wrap in plastic wrap. Refrigerate for 2 hours or until firm.

UNWRAP logs; slice into ¼-inch-thick slices. Place slices on ungreased baking sheets.

BAKE for 5 to 6 minutes or until edges are set. Cool on baking sheets for 2 minutes; remove to wire racks to cool completely. *Makes about 6 dozen cookies*

Jumbo 3-Chip Cookies

4 cups all-purpose flour
1 teaspoon baking powder
1 teaspoon baking soda
1½ cups (3 sticks) butter, softened
1¼ cups granulated sugar
1¼ cups packed brown sugar
2 large eggs
1 tablespoon vanilla extract
1 cup (6 ounces) NESTLÉ TOLL HOUSE Milk Chocolate Morsels
1 cup (6 ounces) NESTLÉ TOLL HOUSE Semi-Sweet Chocolate Morsels
½ cup NESTLÉ TOLL HOUSE Premier White Morsels
1 cup chopped nuts

PREHEAT oven to 375°F.

COMBINE flour, baking powder and baking soda in medium bowl. Beat butter, granulated sugar and brown sugar in large mixer bowl until creamy. Beat in eggs and vanilla extract. Gradually beat in flour mixture. Stir in morsels and nuts. Drop by level ¼-cup measure 2 inches apart onto ungreased baking sheets.

BAKE for 12 to 14 minutes or until light golden brown. Cool on baking sheets for 2 minutes; remove to wire racks to cool completely.   *Makes about 2 dozen cookies*

Pumpkin Orange Cookies

2½ cups all-purpose flour
½ teaspoon baking soda
½ teaspoon salt
1 cup (2 sticks) butter or margarine, softened
1 cup granulated sugar
½ cup packed brown sugar
1 large egg
1 can (15 ounces) LIBBY'S 100% Pure Pumpkin
2 tablespoons orange juice
1 teaspoon grated orange peel
½ cup chopped nuts (optional)
   Orange Glaze (recipe follows)

PREHEAT oven to 375°F.

COMBINE flour, baking soda and salt in medium bowl. Combine butter, granulated sugar and brown sugar in large mixer bowl; beat until creamy. Add egg, pumpkin, orange juice and orange peel; beat until combined. Gradually add flour mixture; beat until combined. Stir in nuts. Drop by rounded tablespoon onto ungreased baking sheets.

BAKE for 12 to 14 minutes or until edges are set. Remove to wire racks to cool completely. Spread each cookie with about ½ teaspoon Orange Glaze.

Makes about 4 dozen cookies

Orange Glaze
COMBINE 1½ cups sifted powdered sugar, 2 to 3 tablespoons orange juice and ½ teaspoon grated orange peel in medium bowl until smooth.

Milk Chocolate Oatmeal Cookies

1¼ cups all-purpose flour
½ teaspoon baking powder
½ teaspoon baking soda
½ teaspoon ground cinnamon
¼ teaspoon salt
¾ cup (1½ sticks) butter or margarine, softened
¾ cup packed brown sugar
⅓ cup granulated sugar
1½ teaspoons vanilla extract
1 large egg
2 tablespoons milk
1¾ cups (11.5-ounce package) NESTLÉ TOLL HOUSE Milk Chocolate Morsels
1 cup quick or old-fashioned oats
½ cup raisins (optional)

PREHEAT oven to 375°F.

COMBINE flour, baking powder, baking soda, cinnamon and salt in small bowl. Beat butter, brown sugar, granulated sugar and vanilla extract in large mixer bowl until creamy. Beat in egg. Gradually beat in flour mixture and milk. Stir in morsels, oats and raisins. Drop by rounded tablespoon onto ungreased baking sheets.

BAKE for 10 to 14 minutes or until edges are crisp but centers are still soft. Cool on baking sheets for 2 minutes; remove to wire racks to cool completely.

Makes about 3 dozen cookies

Mini Chip Snowball Cookies

1½ cups (3 sticks) butter or margarine, softened
¾ cup powdered sugar
1 tablespoon vanilla extract
½ teaspoon salt
3 cups all-purpose flour
2 cups (12-ounce package) NESTLÉ TOLL HOUSE Semi-Sweet Chocolate Mini Morsels
½ cup finely chopped nuts
Powdered sugar

PREHEAT oven to 375°F.

BEAT butter, sugar, vanilla extract and salt in large mixer bowl until creamy. Gradually beat in flour; stir in morsels and nuts. Shape level tablespoons of dough into 1¼-inch balls. Place on ungreased baking sheets.

BAKE for 10 to 12 minutes or until cookies are set and lightly browned. Remove from oven. Sift powdered sugar over hot cookies on baking sheets. Cool on baking sheets for 10 minutes; remove to wire racks to cool completely. Sprinkle with additional powdered sugar, if desired. Store in airtight containers.

Makes about 5 dozen cookies

tip

To sprinkle cookies or other desserts with powdered sugar, place powdered sugar in a small, fine-meshed strainer and gently tap or shake the strainer over the cookies.

Oatmeal Scotchies

1¼ cups all-purpose flour
1 teaspoon baking soda
½ teaspoon ground cinnamon
½ teaspoon salt
1 cup (2 sticks) butter or margarine, softened
¾ cup granulated sugar
¾ cup packed brown sugar
2 large eggs
1 teaspoon vanilla extract or grated peel of 1 orange
3 cups quick or old-fashioned oats
1⅔ cups (11-ounce package) NESTLÉ TOLL HOUSE Butterscotch Flavored
    Morsels

PREHEAT oven to 375°F.

COMBINE flour, baking soda, cinnamon and salt in small bowl. Beat butter, granulated sugar, brown sugar, eggs and vanilla extract in large mixer bowl. Gradually beat in flour mixture. Stir in oats and morsels. Drop by rounded tablespoon onto ungreased baking sheets.

BAKE for 7 to 8 minutes for chewy cookies or 9 to 10 minutes for crispy cookies. Cool on baking sheets for 2 minutes; remove to wire racks to cool completely.

Makes about 4 dozen cookies

Pan Cookie Variation
GREASE 15 × 10-inch jelly-roll pan. Spread dough into prepared pan. Bake for 18 to 22 minutes or until light brown. Cool completely in pan on wire rack. Makes 4 dozen bars.

Chocolate Almond Biscotti

2 cups (12-ounce package) NESTLÉ TOLL HOUSE Semi-Sweet
   Chocolate Morsels, *divided*
2 cups all-purpose flour
¼ cup NESTLÉ TOLL HOUSE Baking Cocoa
1½ teaspoons baking powder
¼ teaspoon baking soda
¼ teaspoon salt
½ cup granulated sugar
½ cup packed brown sugar
¼ cup (½ stick) butter or margarine, softened
½ teaspoon vanilla extract
½ teaspoon almond extract
3 large eggs
1 cup slivered almonds, toasted
   Chocolate Coating (recipe follows), optional

PREHEAT oven to 325°F. Grease 1 large or 2 small baking sheet(s).

MICROWAVE *1 cup* morsels in small, microwave-safe bowl on HIGH (100%) power for 1 minute; stir. Microwave at additional 10- to 20-second intervals, stirring until smooth. Cool to room temperature.

COMBINE flour, cocoa, baking powder, baking soda and salt in medium bowl. Beat granulated sugar, brown sugar, butter, vanilla extract and almond extract until crumbly. Add eggs, one at a time, beating well after each addition. Beat in melted chocolate. Gradually beat in flour mixture. Stir in nuts. Refrigerate for 15 minutes or until firm.

SHAPE dough with floured hands into two 9 × 3-inch logs on prepared baking sheet(s).

BAKE for 40 to 50 minutes or until wooden pick inserted in center of each log comes out clean. Cool on baking sheets for 15 minutes. Slide logs onto cutting board and cut diagonally into ¾-inch slices. Return to baking sheet(s) cut side down. Bake, turning biscotti over halfway through, for 20 minutes or until dry. Remove to wire racks to cool completely.

LINE baking sheet(s) with wax paper.

DIP biscotti halfway into Chocolate Coating; shake off excess. Place on prepared baking sheet(s). Refrigerate for 10 minutes or until chocolate is set. Store in airtight containers in cool place or in refrigerator.   *Makes about 2½ dozen cookies*

Chocolate Coating
MICROWAVE *remaining* morsels and 2 tablespoons vegetable shortening in medium, microwave-safe bowl on HIGH (100%) power for 1 minute; stir. Microwave at 10- to 20-second intervals, stirring until smooth.

Choc-Oat-Chip Cookies

1¾ cups all-purpose flour
1 teaspoon baking soda
½ teaspoon salt (optional)
1¼ cups packed brown sugar
1 cup (2 sticks) butter or margarine, softened
½ cup granulated sugar
2 large eggs
2 tablespoons milk
2 teaspoons vanilla extract
2½ cups quick or old-fashioned oats
2 cups (12-ounce package) NESTLÉ TOLL HOUSE Semi-Sweet
    Chocolate Morsels
1 cup coarsely chopped nuts (optional)

PREHEAT oven to 375°F.

COMBINE flour, baking soda and salt in small bowl. Beat brown sugar, butter and granulated sugar in large mixer bowl until creamy. Beat in eggs, milk and vanilla extract. Gradually beat in flour mixture. Stir in oats, morsels and nuts; mix well. Drop by rounded tablespoon onto ungreased baking sheets.

BAKE for 9 to 10 minutes for chewy cookies or 12 to 13 minutes for crispy cookies. Cool on baking sheets for 1 minute; remove to wire racks to cool completely.

Makes about 4 dozen cookies

Milk Chocolate Florentine Cookies

⅔ cup butter
2 cups quick oats
1 cup granulated sugar
⅔ cup all-purpose flour
¼ cup light or dark corn syrup
¼ cup milk
1 teaspoon vanilla extract
¼ teaspoon salt
1¾ cups (11.5-ounce package) NESTLÉ TOLL HOUSE Milk Chocolate Morsels

PREHEAT oven to 375°F. Line baking sheets with foil.

MELT butter in medium saucepan; remove from heat. Stir in oats, sugar, flour, corn syrup, milk, vanilla extract and salt; mix well. Drop by level teaspoon, about 3 inches apart, onto prepared baking sheets. Spread thinly with rubber spatula.

BAKE for 6 to 8 minutes or until golden brown. Cool completely on baking sheets on wire racks. Peel foil from cookies.

MICROWAVE morsels in medium, microwave-safe bowl on MEDIUM-HIGH (70%) power for 1 minute; stir. Microwave at additional 10- to 20-second intervals, stirring until smooth. Spread thin layer of melted chocolate onto flat side of *half* the cookies. Top with *remaining* cookies. *Makes about 3½ dozen sandwich cookies*

Chocolate Gingerbread Boys and Girls

2 cups (12-ounce package) NESTLÉ TOLL HOUSE Semi-Sweet Chocolate
   Morsels, *divided*
2¾ cups all-purpose flour
1 teaspoon baking soda
½ teaspoon salt
½ teaspoon ground ginger
½ teaspoon ground cinnamon
3 tablespoons butter or margarine, softened
3 tablespoons granulated sugar
½ cup molasses
¼ cup water
1 container (16 ounces) prepared vanilla frosting, colored as desired, or colored
   icing in tubes

MICROWAVE *1½ cups* morsels in medium, microwave-safe bowl on HIGH (100%) power for 1 minute; stir. Microwave at additional 10- to 20-second intervals, stirring until smooth; cool to room temperature.

COMBINE flour, baking soda, salt, ginger and cinnamon in medium bowl. Beat butter and sugar in small mixer bowl until creamy; beat in molasses and melted chocolate. Gradually add flour mixture alternately with water, beating until smooth. Cover; refrigerate for 1 hour or until firm.

PREHEAT oven to 350°F.

ROLL *half* of dough to ¼-inch thickness on floured surface with floured rolling pin. Cut dough into gingerbread boy and girl shapes using cookie cutters or a stencil. Place on ungreased baking sheets. Repeat with *remaining* dough.

BAKE for 5 to 6 minutes or until edges are set but centers are still slightly soft. Cool on baking sheets for 2 minutes; remove to wire racks to cool completely.

PLACE *remaining* morsels in *heavy-duty* resealable plastic food storage bag. Microwave on HIGH (100%) power for 30 to 45 seconds; knead. Microwave for 10 seconds; knead until smooth. Cut tiny corner from bag; squeeze to pipe chocolate. Decorate with piped frosting or icing.   *Makes about 2½ dozen cookies*

Frosted Double Chocolate Cookies

2 cups (12-ounce package) NESTLÉ TOLL HOUSE Semi-Sweet Chocolate
  Morsels, *divided*
1¼ cups all-purpose flour
¾ teaspoon baking soda
½ teaspoon salt
½ cup (1 stick) butter or margarine, softened
½ cup packed brown sugar
¼ cup granulated sugar
1 teaspoon vanilla extract
1 large egg
½ cup chopped nuts (optional)
  Chocolate Frosting (recipe follows)

PREHEAT oven to 375°F.

MICROWAVE *¾ cup* morsels in small, microwave-safe bowl on HIGH (100%) power for 1 minute; stir. Microwave at additional 10- to 20-second intervals, stirring until smooth; cool to room temperature. Combine flour, baking soda and salt in small bowl.

BEAT butter, brown sugar, granulated sugar and vanilla extract in large mixer bowl until creamy. Beat in melted chocolate and egg. Gradually beat in flour mixture. Stir in *¾ cup* morsels and nuts. Drop by rounded tablespoon onto ungreased baking sheets.

BAKE for 8 to 9 minutes or until edges are set but centers are still slightly soft. Cool on baking sheets for 3 minutes; remove to wire racks to cool completely. Thinly frost centers of cookies with Chocolate Frosting.   *Makes 2½ dozen cookies*

Chocolate Frosting
MICROWAVE *remaining ½ cup* morsels and 2 tablespoons butter or margarine in medium, microwave-safe bowl on HIGH (100%) power for 30 seconds; stir until smooth. Microwave at additional 10- to 20-second intervals, stirring until smooth. Add 1¼ cups sifted powdered sugar and 2 tablespoons milk; stir until smooth.

Pumpkin Spiced and Iced Cookies

2¼ cups all-purpose flour
1½ teaspoons pumpkin pie spice
  1 teaspoon baking powder
½ teaspoon baking soda
½ teaspoon salt
  1 cup (2 sticks) butter or margarine, softened
  1 cup granulated sugar
  1 can (15 ounces) LIBBY'S 100% Pure Pumpkin
  2 large eggs
  1 teaspoon vanilla extract
  2 cups (12-ounce package) NESTLÉ TOLL HOUSE Semi-Sweet
    Chocolate Morsels
  1 cup chopped walnuts (optional)
    Vanilla Glaze (recipe follows)

PREHEAT oven to 375°F. Grease baking sheets.

COMBINE flour, pumpkin pie spice, baking powder, baking soda and salt in medium bowl. Beat butter and sugar in large mixer bowl until creamy. Beat in pumpkin, eggs and vanilla extract. Gradually beat in flour mixture. Stir in morsels and nuts. Drop by rounded tablespoon onto prepared baking sheets.

BAKE for 15 to 20 minutes or until edges are lightly browned. Cool on baking sheets for 2 minutes; remove to wire rack to cool completely. Spread or drizzle with Vanilla Glaze.

Makes about 5½ dozen cookies

Vanilla Glaze
COMBINE 1 cup powdered sugar, 1 to 1½ tablespoons milk and ½ teaspoon vanilla extract in small bowl; mix well.

Chocolate-Cherry Thumbprints

2 cups (12-ounce package) NESTLÉ TOLL HOUSE Semi-Sweet Chocolate Morsels, *divided*
1¾ cups quick or old-fashioned oats
1½ cups all-purpose flour
¼ cup NESTLÉ TOLL HOUSE Baking Cocoa
1 teaspoon baking powder
¼ teaspoon salt (optional)
¾ cup granulated sugar
⅔ cup butter or margarine, softened
2 large eggs
1 teaspoon vanilla extract
2 cups (two 10-ounce jars) maraschino cherries, drained and patted dry

MICROWAVE *1 cup* morsels in small, microwave-safe bowl on HIGH (100%) power for 1 minute; stir. Microwave at additional 10- to 20-second intervals, stirring until smooth. Combine oats, flour, cocoa, baking powder and salt in medium bowl.

BEAT sugar, butter, eggs and vanilla extract in large mixer bowl until smooth. Beat in melted chocolate. Stir in oat mixture. Cover; refrigerate dough for 1 hour.

PREHEAT oven to 350°F.

SHAPE dough into 1-inch balls. Place 2 inches apart on ungreased baking sheets. Press thumb into tops to make deep depressions. Place maraschino cherry into each depression.

BAKE for 10 to 12 minutes or until set. Cool on baking sheets for 2 minutes; remove to wire racks to cool completely. Melt *remaining* morsels; drizzle over cookies.

Makes about 4 dozen cookies

Chocolate Dipped Brandy Snaps

½ cup (1 stick) butter
½ cup granulated sugar
⅓ cup dark corn syrup
½ teaspoon ground cinnamon
¼ teaspoon ground ginger
1 cup all-purpose flour
2 teaspoons brandy
1 cup (6 ounces) NESTLÉ TOLL HOUSE Semi-Sweet Chocolate Morsels
1 tablespoon vegetable shortening
⅓ cup finely chopped nuts

PREHEAT oven to 300°F.

COMBINE butter, sugar, corn syrup, cinnamon and ginger in medium, *heavy-duty* saucepan over low heat, stirring until smooth. Remove from heat; stir in flour and brandy. Drop by rounded teaspoon onto ungreased baking sheets about 3 inches apart, baking no more than six at a time.

BAKE for 10 to 14 minutes or until deep caramel color. Cool on baking sheets for 10 seconds. Remove from baking sheets and immediately roll around wooden spoon handle; cool completely on wire racks.

LINE baking sheets with wax paper.

MICROWAVE morsels and vegetable shortening in medium, microwave-safe bowl on HIGH (100%) power for 1 minute; stir. Microwave at additional 10- to 20-second intervals, stirring until smooth. Dip cookies halfway in melted chocolate; shake off excess. Sprinkle with nuts; set on prepared baking sheets. Refrigerate for 10 minutes or until chocolate is set. Store in airtight container in refrigerator.

Makes about 3 dozen cookies

Chunky Chocolate Chip Peanut Butter Cookies

1¼ cups all-purpose flour
½ teaspoon baking soda
½ teaspoon ground cinnamon
½ teaspoon salt
¾ cup (1½ sticks) butter or margarine, softened
½ cup packed brown sugar
½ cup granulated sugar
½ cup creamy peanut butter
1 large egg
1 teaspoon vanilla extract
2 cups (12-ounce package) NESTLÉ TOLL HOUSE Semi-Sweet Choco
    Morsels
½ cup coarsely chopped peanuts

PREHEAT oven to 375°F.

COMBINE flour, baking soda, cinnamon and salt in small bowl. Beat butter, brown sugar, granulated sugar and peanut butter in large mixer bowl until creamy. Beat in egg and vanilla extract. Gradually beat in flour mixture. Stir in morsels and peanuts.

DROP by rounded tablespoon onto ungreased baking sheets. Press down slightly to flatten into 2-inch circles.

BAKE for 7 to 10 minutes or until edges are set but centers are still soft. Cool on baking sheets for 4 minutes; remove to wire racks to cool completely.

Makes about 3 dozen cookies

Lemon Nut White Chip Cookies

1½ cups all-purpose flour
¾ teaspoon baking soda
½ teaspoon salt
¾ cup (1½ sticks) butter or margarine, softened
½ cup packed brown sugar
¼ cup granulated sugar
1 large egg
1 tablespoon lemon juice
2 cups (12-ounce package) NESTLÉ TOLL HOUSE Premier White Morsels
1 cup coarsely chopped walnuts or cashew nuts
1 teaspoon grated lemon peel

PREHEAT oven to 375°F.

COMBINE flour, baking soda and salt in small bowl. Beat butter, brown sugar and granulated sugar in large mixer bowl until creamy. Beat in egg and lemon juice; gradually beat in flour mixture. Stir in morsels, nuts and lemon peel. Drop by rounded tablespoon onto ungreased baking sheets.

BAKE for 7 to 10 minutes or until edges are lightly browned. Cool on baking sheets for 3 minutes; remove to wire racks to cool completely.

Makes about 3 dozen cookies

Mini Morsel Meringue Cookies

4 large egg whites
½ teaspoon salt
½ teaspoon cream of tartar
1 cup granulated sugar
2 cups (12-ounce package) NESTLÉ TOLL HOUSE Semi-Sweet Chocolate Mini Morsels

PREHEAT oven to 300°F. Grease baking sheets.

BEAT egg whites, salt and cream of tartar in small mixer bowl until soft peaks form. Gradually add sugar; beat until stiff peaks form. Gently fold in morsels ⅓ cup at a time. Drop by level tablespoon onto prepared baking sheets.

BAKE for 20 to 25 minutes or until meringues are dry and crisp. Cool on baking sheets for 2 minutes; remove to wire racks to cool completely. Store in airtight containers.

Makes about 5 dozen cookies

Oatmeal-Chip Cookie Mix in a Jar

⅔ cup all-purpose flour
½ teaspoon baking soda
½ teaspoon ground cinnamon
¼ teaspoon salt
⅓ cup packed brown sugar
⅓ cup granulated sugar
¾ cup NESTLÉ TOLL HOUSE Semi-Sweet Chocolate or Butterscotch Flavored
    Morsels
1½ cups quick or old-fashioned oats
½ cup chopped nuts

COMBINE flour, baking soda, cinnamon and salt in small bowl. Place flour mixture in 1-quart jar. Layer remaining ingredients in order listed above, pressing firmly after each layer. Seal with lid and decorate with fabric and ribbon.

Recipe to Attach

Beat ½ cup (1 stick) softened butter or margarine, 1 large egg and ½ teaspoon vanilla extract in large mixer bowl until blended. Add cookie mix; mix well, breaking up any clumps. Drop by rounded tablespoon onto ungreased baking sheets. Bake in preheated 375°F. oven for 8 to 10 minutes. Cool on baking sheets for 2 minutes; remove to wire racks. Makes about 2 dozen cookies.

Brownies & Bars

No-Bake Chocolate Peanut Butter Bars

2 cups peanut butter, *divided*
¾ cup (1½ sticks) butter, softened
2 cups powdered sugar, *divided*
3 cups graham cracker crumbs
2 cups (12-ounce package) NESTLÉ TOLL HOUSE Semi-Sweet Chocolate
   Mini Morsels, *divided*

GREASE 13 × 9-inch baking pan.

BEAT 1¼ cups peanut butter and butter in large mixer bowl until creamy. Gradually beat in *1 cup* powdered sugar. With hands or wooden spoon, work in *remaining* powdered sugar, graham cracker crumbs and *½ cup* morsels. Press evenly into prepared pan. Smooth top with spatula.

MELT *remaining* peanut butter and *remaining* morsels in medium, *heavy-duty* saucepan over *lowest possible heat*, stirring constantly, until smooth. Spread over graham cracker crust in pan. Refrigerate for at least 1 hour or until chocolate is firm; cut into bars. Store in refrigerator.   *Makes about 5 dozen bars*

Razz-Ma-Tazz Bars

½ cup (1 stick) butter or margarine
2 cups (12-ounce package) NESTLÉ TOLL HOUSE Premier White Morsels, *divided*
2 large eggs
½ cup granulated sugar
1 cup all-purpose flour
½ teaspoon salt
½ teaspoon almond extract
½ cup seedless raspberry jam
¼ cup toasted sliced almonds

PREHEAT oven to 325°F. Grease and sugar 9-inch-square baking pan.

MELT butter in medium, microwave-safe bowl on HIGH (100%) power for 1 minute; stir. Add *1 cup* morsels; let stand. Do not stir.

BEAT eggs in large mixer bowl until foamy. Add sugar; beat until light lemon colored, about 5 minutes. Stir in morsel-butter mixture. Add flour, salt and almond extract; mix at low speed until combined. Spread ⅔ of batter into prepared pan.

BAKE for 15 to 17 minutes or until light golden brown around edges. Remove from oven to wire rack.

HEAT jam in small, microwave-safe bowl on HIGH (100%) power for 30 seconds; stir. Spread jam over warm crust. Stir *remaining* morsels into *remaining* batter. Drop spoonfuls of batter over jam. Sprinkle with almonds.

BAKE for 25 to 30 minutes or until edges are browned. Cool completely in pan on wire rack. Cut into bars.

Makes 16 bars

Chocolate Amaretto Bars

Crust

    2 cups all-purpose flour
    ¾ cup (1½ sticks) butter or margarine, cut into pieces, softened
    ⅓ cup packed brown sugar

Filling

    4 large eggs
    ¾ cup light corn syrup
    ¾ cup granulated sugar
    ¼ cup amaretto liqueur or ½ teaspoon almond extract
    2 tablespoons butter or margarine, melted
    1 tablespoon cornstarch
    2 cups (about 7 ounces) sliced almonds
    2 cups (12-ounce package) NESTLÉ TOLL HOUSE Semi-Sweet Chocolate Morsels, *divided*
    Chocolate Drizzle (recipe follows), optional

PREHEAT oven to 350°F. Grease 13 × 9-inch baking pan.

For Crust

BEAT flour, butter and brown sugar in large mixer bowl until crumbly. Press into prepared baking pan. Bake for 12 to 15 minutes or until golden brown.

For Filling

BEAT eggs, corn syrup, granulated sugar, liqueur, butter and cornstarch in medium bowl with wire whisk. Stir in almonds and *1⅔ cups* morsels. Pour over hot crust; spread evenly. Bake for 25 to 30 minutes or until center is set. Cool in pan on wire rack.

Chocolate Drizzle

PLACE *remaining* morsels in *heavy-duty* resealable plastic food storage bag. Microwave on HIGH (100%) power for 30 to 45 seconds; knead. Microwave at 10- to 20-second intervals, kneading until smooth. Cut tiny corner from bag; squeeze to drizzle over bars. Refrigerate for few minutes to firm chocolate before cutting into bars.

Makes 2½ dozen bars

White Chip Island Blondies

    1 cup plus 2 tablespoons all-purpose flour
    1 teaspoon baking powder
    ¼ teaspoon salt
    ¾ cup packed light brown sugar
    ⅓ cup butter or margarine, softened
    ½ teaspoon vanilla extract
    1 large egg
    1 cup (6 ounces) NESTLÉ TOLL HOUSE Premier White Morsels
    ½ cup coarsely chopped macadamia nuts
    ½ cup toasted coconut

PREHEAT oven to 350°F. Grease 9-inch-square baking pan.

COMBINE flour, baking powder and salt in medium bowl. Beat sugar, butter and vanilla extract in large mixer bowl until creamy. Beat in egg. Gradually beat in flour mixture. Stir in morsels, nuts and coconut. Press into prepared baking pan.

BAKE for 20 to 25 minutes or until golden brown. Cool completely in pan on wire rack. Cut into bars. *Makes about 16 bars*

Peanut Butter Chocolate Layer Bars

    2 cups (about 20) crushed peanut butter sandwich cookies
    3 tablespoons butter or margarine, melted
 1¼ cups lightly salted dry-roasted peanuts, chopped
    1 cup (6 ounces) NESTLÉ TOLL HOUSE Semi-Sweet Chocolate Morsels
    1 cup flaked coconut
    1 can (14 ounces) NESTLÉ CARNATION Sweetened Condensed Milk

PREHEAT oven to 350°F. Grease 13 × 9-inch baking pan.

COMBINE cookie crumbs and butter in small bowl; press onto bottom of prepared pan. Layer nuts, morsels and coconut over crumb mixture. Drizzle sweetened condensed milk evenly over top.

BAKE for 20 to 25 minutes or until coconut is golden brown. Cool completely in pan on wire rack. Cut into bars. *Makes 2 dozen bars*

Layers of Love Chocolate Brownies

¾ cup all-purpose flour
¾ cup NESTLÉ TOLL HOUSE Baking Cocoa
¼ teaspoon salt
½ cup (1 stick) butter, cut in pieces
½ cup granulated sugar
½ cup packed brown sugar
3 large eggs, *divided*
2 teaspoons vanilla extract
1 cup chopped pecans
¾ cup NESTLÉ TOLL HOUSE Premier White Morsels
½ cup caramel ice cream topping
¾ cup NESTLÉ TOLL HOUSE Semi-Sweet Chocolate Morsels

PREHEAT oven to 350°F. Grease 8-inch-square baking pan.

COMBINE flour, cocoa and salt in small bowl. Beat butter, granulated sugar and brown sugar in large mixer bowl until creamy. Add *2 eggs*, one at a time, beating well after each addition. Add vanilla extract; mix well. Gradually beat in flour mixture. Reserve ¾ *cup* batter. Spread *remaining* batter into prepared baking pan. Sprinkle pecans and white morsels over batter. Drizzle caramel topping over top. Beat *remaining* egg and *reserved* batter in same large bowl until light in color. Stir in semi-sweet morsels. Spread evenly over caramel topping.

BAKE for 30 to 35 minutes or until center is set. Cool completely in pan on wire rack. Cut into squares. *Makes 16 brownies*

Lemon Bars

Crust
>   2 cups all-purpose flour
>   ½ cup powdered sugar
>   1 cup (2 sticks) butter or margarine, softened

Filling
>   1 can (14 ounces) NESTLÉ CARNATION Sweetened Condensed Milk
>   4 large eggs
>   ⅔ cup lemon juice
>   1 tablespoon all-purpose flour
>   1 teaspoon baking powder
>   ¼ teaspoon salt
>   4 drops yellow food coloring (optional)
>   1 tablespoon grated lemon peel
>   Sifted powdered sugar (optional)

PREHEAT oven to 350°F.

For Crust
COMBINE flour and sugar in medium bowl. Cut in butter with pastry blender or two knives until mixture is crumbly. Press lightly onto bottom and halfway up sides of ungreased 13 × 9-inch baking pan.

BAKE for 20 minutes.

For Filling
BEAT sweetened condensed milk and eggs in large mixer bowl until fluffy. Beat in lemon juice, flour, baking powder, salt and food coloring just until blended. Fold in lemon peel; pour over crust.

BAKE for 20 to 25 minutes or until filling is set and crust is golden brown. Cool in pan on wire rack. Refrigerate for about 2 hours. Cut into bars; sprinkle with powdered sugar.

Makes 4 dozen bars

Date Bars

1 package (8 ounces) chopped dates
¾ cup NESTLÉ CARNATION Evaporated Milk
2 tablespoons granulated sugar
1 teaspoon vanilla extract
½ cup (1 stick) butter or margarine, softened
½ cup packed light brown sugar
1 cup all-purpose flour
¾ cup quick oats
½ teaspoon baking soda
½ teaspoon salt
½ teaspoon ground cinnamon

PREHEAT oven to 400°F. Grease 8-inch-square baking pan.

COMBINE dates, evaporated milk, granulated sugar and vanilla extract in medium saucepan. Cook over medium-low heat, stirring occasionally, for 8 to 10 minutes or until thickened. Remove from heat.

BEAT butter and brown sugar in large mixer bowl until creamy. Beat in flour, oats, baking soda, salt and cinnamon. With floured fingers, press *half* of crust mixture onto bottom of prepared baking pan. Spread date filling over crust. Top with *remaining* crust.

BAKE for 20 to 25 minutes or until golden. Serve warm. Cut into bars.

Makes 16 bars

For perfect results when baking cookies and bars, check for doneness at the minimum baking time stated in the recipe. Cookies do continue to bake slightly after they have been removed from the oven. For chewy bars and cookies, take them out when they are still somewhat light in color.

Chocolate Crumb Bars

  1 cup (2 sticks) butter or margarine, softened
1¾ cups all-purpose flour
  ½ cup granulated sugar
  ¼ teaspoon salt
  2 cups (12-ounce package) NESTLÉ TOLL HOUSE Semi-Sweet
     Chocolate Morsels, *divided*
  1 can (14 ounces) NESTLÉ CARNATION Sweetened Condensed Milk
  1 teaspoon vanilla extract
  1 cup chopped walnuts (optional)

PREHEAT oven to 350°F. Grease 13 × 9-inch baking pan.

BEAT butter in large mixer bowl until creamy. Beat in flour, sugar and salt until crumbly. With floured fingers, press *2 cups* crumb mixture onto bottom of prepared baking pan; reserve *remaining* mixture.

BAKE for 10 to 12 minutes or until edges are golden brown.

COMBINE *1 cup* morsels and sweetened condensed milk in small, *heavy-duty* saucepan. Warm over low heat, stirring until smooth. Stir in vanilla extract. Spread over hot crust.

STIR nuts and *remaining* morsels into *reserved* crumb mixture; sprinkle over chocolate filling. Bake for 25 to 30 minutes or until center is set. Cool in pan on wire rack. Cut into bars.   *Makes 2½ dozen bars*

Chunky Pecan Pie Bars

Crust
  1½ cups all-purpose flour
  ½ cup (1 stick) butter or margarine, softened
  ¼ cup packed brown sugar

Filling
  3 large eggs
  ¾ cup corn syrup
  ¾ cup granulated sugar
  2 tablespoons butter or margarine, melted
  1 teaspoon vanilla extract
1¾ cups (11.5-ounce package) NESTLÉ TOLL HOUSE Semi-Sweet
    Chocolate Chunks
1½ cups coarsely chopped pecans

PREHEAT oven to 350°F. Grease 13 × 9-inch baking pan.

For Crust
BEAT flour, butter and brown sugar in small mixer bowl until crumbly. Press into prepared baking pan.

BAKE for 12 to 15 minutes or until lightly browned.

For Filling
BEAT eggs, corn syrup, granulated sugar, butter and vanilla extract in medium bowl with wire whisk. Stir in chunks and nuts. Pour evenly over baked crust.

BAKE for 25 to 30 minutes or until set. Cool completely in pan on wire rack. Cut into bars.
Makes about 3 dozen bars

Premier Cheesecake Cranberry Bars

2 cups all-purpose flour
1½ cups quick or old-fashioned oats
¼ cup packed light brown sugar
1 cup (2 sticks) butter or margarine, softened
2 cups (12-ounce package) NESTLÉ TOLL HOUSE Premier White Morsels
1 package (8 ounces) cream cheese, softened
1 can (14 ounces) NESTLÉ CARNATION Sweetened Condensed Milk
¼ cup lemon juice
1 teaspoon vanilla extract
1 can (16 ounces) whole-berry cranberry sauce
2 tablespoons cornstarch

PREHEAT oven to 350°F. Grease 13 × 9-inch baking pan.

COMBINE flour, oats and brown sugar in large bowl. Add butter; mix until crumbly. Stir in morsels. Reserve *2½ cups* morsel mixture for topping. With floured fingers, press *remaining* mixture into prepared pan.

BEAT cream cheese in large mixer bowl until creamy. Add sweetened condensed milk, lemon juice and vanilla extract; mix until smooth. Pour over crust. Combine cranberry sauce and cornstarch in medium bowl. Spoon over cream cheese mixture. Sprinkle *reserved* morsel mixture over cranberry mixture.

BAKE for 35 to 40 minutes or until center is set. Cool completely in pan on wire rack. Cover; refrigerate until serving time (up to 1 day). Cut into bars.

Makes 2½ dozen bars

Moist and Minty Brownies

Brownies
1¼ cups all-purpose flour
½ teaspoon baking soda
¼ teaspoon salt
¾ cup granulated sugar
½ cup (1 stick) butter or margarine
2 tablespoons water
1½ cups (9 ounces) NESTLÉ TOLL HOUSE Semi-Sweet Chocolate Morsels,
  divided
½ teaspoon peppermint extract
½ teaspoon vanilla extract
2 large eggs

Frosting
1 container (16 ounces) prepared vanilla frosting
1 tube (4½ ounces) chocolate decorating icing

For Brownies
PREHEAT oven to 350°F. Grease 9-inch-square baking pan.

COMBINE flour, baking soda and salt in small bowl. Combine sugar, butter and water in medium saucepan. Bring *just to a boil* over medium heat, stirring constantly; remove from heat. (Or, combine sugar, butter and water in medium, microwave-safe bowl. Microwave on HIGH (100%) power for 3 minutes, stirring halfway through cooking time.) Stir until smooth.

ADD *1 cup* morsels, peppermint extract and vanilla extract; stir until smooth. Add eggs, one at a time, stirring well after each addition. Stir in flour mixture and *remaining* morsels. Spread into prepared baking pan.

BAKE for 20 to 30 minutes or until center is set. Cool completely (center will sink) in pan on wire rack.

For Frosting
SPREAD vanilla frosting over brownie. Squeeze chocolate icing in parallel lines over frosting. Drag wooden pick through chocolate icing to feather. Let stand until frosting is set. Cut into squares.   *Makes about 16 brownies*

Fruit and Chocolate Dream Bars

Crust
  1¼ cups all-purpose flour
  ½ cup granulated sugar
  ½ cup (1 stick) butter or margarine

Topping
  ⅔ cup all-purpose flour
  ½ cup chopped pecans
  ⅓ cup packed brown sugar
  6 tablespoons butter or margarine, softened
  ½ cup raspberry or strawberry jam
  1¾ cups (11.5-ounce package) NESTLÉ TOLL HOUSE Milk Chocolate Morsels

PREHEAT oven to 375°F. Grease 9-inch-square baking pan.

For Crust
COMBINE flour and granulated sugar in medium bowl. Cut in butter with pastry blender or two knives until mixture resembles coarse crumbs. Press onto bottom of prepared baking pan.

BAKE for 18 to 22 minutes or until set but not brown.

For Topping
COMBINE flour, nuts and brown sugar in small bowl. Cut in butter with pastry blender or two knives until mixture resembles coarse crumbs.

SPREAD jam over hot crust. Sprinkle with morsels and topping.

BAKE for 15 to 20 minutes or until golden brown. Cool completely in pan on wire rack. Cut into bars.   *Makes 2½ dozen bars*

Easy Double Chocolate Chip Brownies

2 cups (12-ounce package) NESTLÉ TOLL HOUSE Semi-Sweet
Chocolate Morsels, *divided*
½ cup (1 stick) butter or margarine, cut into pieces
3 large eggs
1¼ cups all-purpose flour
1 cup granulated sugar
1 teaspoon vanilla extract
¼ teaspoon baking soda
½ cup chopped nuts

PREHEAT oven to 350°F. Grease 13 × 9-inch baking pan.

MELT *1 cup* morsels and butter in large, *heavy-duty* saucepan over low heat; stir until smooth. Remove from heat. Stir in eggs. Stir in flour, sugar, vanilla extract and baking soda. Stir in *remaining* morsels and nuts. Spread into prepared baking pan.

BAKE for 18 to 22 minutes or until wooden pick inserted in center comes out slightly sticky. Cool completely in pan on wire rack. Cut into bars.

Makes 2 dozen brownies

tip

Lining a baking pan with heavy-duty aluminum foil makes it easy to remove brownies or bars from the pan, and it also makes cleaning up a breeze. Simply let the brownies or bars cool completely in the pan, then lift them out and peel away the foil.

Swirled Peanut Butter Chocolate Cheesecake Bars

Crust
   2 cups graham cracker crumbs
   ½ cup (1 stick) butter or margarine, melted
   ⅓ cup granulated sugar

Filling
   2 packages (8 ounces *each*) cream cheese, softened
   1 cup granulated sugar
   ¼ cup all-purpose flour
   1 can (12 fluid ounces) NESTLÉ CARNATION Evaporated Milk
   2 large eggs
   1 tablespoon vanilla extract
   1 cup (6 ounces) NESTLÉ TOLL HOUSE Peanut Butter & Milk Chocolate
      Morsels

PREHEAT oven to 325°F.

For Crust
COMBINE graham cracker crumbs, butter and sugar in medium bowl; press onto bottom of ungreased 13 × 9-inch baking pan.

For Filling
BEAT cream cheese, sugar and flour in large mixer bowl until smooth. Gradually beat in evaporated milk, eggs and vanilla extract.

MICROWAVE morsels in medium, microwave-safe bowl on MEDIUM-HIGH (70%) power for 1 minute; stir. Microwave at additional 10- to 20-second intervals, stirring until smooth. Stir *1 cup* cream cheese mixture into chocolate. Pour *remaining* cream cheese mixture over crust. Pour chocolate mixture over cream cheese mixture. Swirl mixtures with spoon, pulling plain cream cheese mixture up to surface.

BAKE for 40 to 45 minutes or until set. Cool completely in pan on wire rack; refrigerate until firm. Cut into bars.   *Makes 15 bars*

Chocolate Brownies

¾ cup granulated sugar
½ cup (1 stick) butter or margarine
2 tablespoons water
4 bars (8-ounce box) NESTLÉ TOLL HOUSE Semi-Sweet Chocolate Baking Bars, broken into pieces
2 large eggs
2 teaspoons vanilla extract
1 cup all-purpose flour
¼ teaspoon baking soda
¼ teaspoon salt
½ cup chopped nuts (optional)

PREHEAT oven to 350°F. Grease 13 × 9-inch baking pan.

MICROWAVE sugar, butter and water in large, microwave-safe bowl on HIGH (100%) power for 3 minutes or until mixture boils, stirring once. Add baking bars; stir until melted. Add eggs, one at a time, stirring well after each addition. Stir in vanilla extract. Add flour, baking soda and salt; stir well. Stir in nuts. Pour into prepared baking pan.

BAKE for 16 to 20 minutes or until wooden pick inserted in center comes out still slightly sticky. Cool completely in pan on wire rack. Cut into bars.

Makes about 2 dozen brownies

Saucepan Method
HEAT sugar, butter and water in medium saucepan *just to a boil*, stirring constantly. Remove from heat. Add baking bars; stir until melted. Proceed as above.

Scotcheroos

Nonstick cooking spray
1½ cups creamy peanut butter
1 cup granulated sugar
1 cup light corn syrup
6 cups toasted rice cereal
1⅔ cups (11-ounce package) NESTLÉ TOLL HOUSE Butterscotch Flavored Morsels
1 cup (6 ounces) NESTLÉ TOLL HOUSE Semi-Sweet Chocolate Morsels

COAT 13 × 9-inch baking pan with cooking spray.

COMBINE peanut butter, sugar and corn syrup in large saucepan. Cook over medium-low heat, stirring frequently, until melted. Remove from heat. Add cereal; stir until thoroughly coated. Press onto bottom of prepared baking pan.

MICROWAVE butterscotch morsels and semi-sweet chocolate morsels in large, microwave-safe bowl on HIGH (100%) power for 1 minute; stir. Microwave at additional 10- to 20-second intervals, stirring until smooth. Spread over cereal mixture.

REFRIGERATE for 15 to 20 minutes or until topping is firm. Cut into bars.

Makes 2½ dozen bars

tip

Before measuring corn syrup or other sticky liquids, lightly coat your measuring cup with nonstick cooking spray—the liquid will slide right out instead of clinging to the side of the cup.

Chocolatey Raspberry Crumb Bars

   1 cup (2 sticks) butter or margarine, softened
   2 cups all-purpose flour
   ½ cup packed light brown sugar
   ¼ teaspoon salt
   2 cups (12-ounce package) NESTLÉ TOLL HOUSE Semi-Sweet
       Chocolate Morsels, *divided*
   1 can (14 ounces) NESTLÉ CARNATION Sweetened Condensed Milk
   ½ cup chopped nuts (optional)
   ⅓ cup seedless raspberry jam

PREHEAT oven to 350°F. Grease 13 × 9-inch baking pan.

BEAT butter in large mixer bowl until creamy. Beat in flour, sugar and salt until crumbly. With floured fingers, press *1¾ cups* crumb mixture onto bottom of prepared baking pan; reserve *remaining* mixture.

BAKE for 10 to 12 minutes or until edges are golden brown.

MICROWAVE *1 cup* morsels and sweetened condensed milk in medium microwave-safe bowl on HIGH (100%) power for 1 minute; stir. Microwave at additional 10- to 20-second intervals, stirring until smooth. Spread over hot crust.

STIR nuts into *reserved* flour mixture; sprinkle over chocolate layer. Drop teaspoonfuls of raspberry jam over flour mixture. Sprinkle with *remaining* morsels.

BAKE for 25 to 30 minutes or until center is set. Cool in pan on wire rack. Cut into bars.   *Makes 3 dozen bars*

Butterscotch Cream Cheese Bars

1⅔ cups (11-ounce package) NESTLÉ TOLL HOUSE Butterscotch Flavored
    Morsels
 6 tablespoons butter or margarine
 2 cups graham cracker crumbs
 2 cups chopped walnuts
 2 packages (8 ounces *each*) cream cheese, softened
½ cup granulated sugar
 4 large eggs
¼ cup all-purpose flour
 2 tablespoons lemon juice

PREHEAT oven to 350°F.

MICROWAVE morsels and butter in medium, microwave-safe bowl on MEDIUM-HIGH (70%) power for 1 minute; stir. Microwave at additional 10- to 20-second intervals, stirring until smooth. Stir in crumbs and nuts. Reserve *2 cups* crumb mixture; press *remaining* mixture into ungreased 15 × 10-inch jelly-roll pan.

BAKE for 12 minutes.

BEAT cream cheese and sugar in large mixer bowl until creamy. Add eggs, one at a time, beating well after each addition. Beat in flour and lemon juice. Pour over crust; sprinkle with *reserved* crumb mixture.

BAKE for 20 to 25 minutes or until set. Cool in pan on wire rack. Cut into bars or diamonds; refrigerate.

Makes about 4 dozen bars

Chewy Butterscotch Brownies

2½ cups all-purpose flour
  1 teaspoon baking powder
½ teaspoon salt
  1 cup (2 sticks) butter or margarine, softened
1¾ cups packed brown sugar
  1 tablespoon vanilla extract
  2 large eggs
1⅔ cups (11-ounce package) NESTLÉ TOLL HOUSE Butterscotch Flavored
      Morsels, *divided*
  1 cup chopped nuts

PREHEAT oven to 350°F.

COMBINE flour, baking powder and salt in medium bowl. Beat butter, sugar and vanilla extract in large mixer bowl until creamy. Beat in eggs. Gradually beat in flour mixture. Stir in *1 cup* morsels and nuts. Spread into ungreased 13 × 9-inch baking pan. Sprinkle with *remaining* morsels.

BAKE for 30 to 40 minutes or until wooden pick inserted in center comes out clean. Cool in pan on wire rack. Cut into bars.   *Makes about 4 dozen brownies*

tip

Brown sugar that has hardened can be softened quickly in the microwave. Place 1 cup sugar in a microwave-safe dish; cover with plastic wrap and heat on HIGH (100%) power for 30 to 45 seconds. Stir and repeat if necessary.

Peanutty Gooey Bars

Crust
>   2 cups chocolate graham cracker crumbs
>   ½ cup (1 stick) butter or margarine, melted
>   ⅓ cup granulated sugar

Topping
>   1⅔ cups (11-ounce package) NESTLÉ TOLL HOUSE Peanut Butter & Milk
>   Chocolate Morsels, *divided*
>   1 can (14 ounces) NESTLÉ CARNATION Sweetened Condensed Milk
>   1 teaspoon vanilla extract
>   1 cup coarsely chopped peanuts

PREHEAT oven to 350°F.

For Crust
COMBINE graham cracker crumbs, butter and sugar in medium bowl; press onto bottom of ungreased 13 × 9-inch baking pan.

For Topping
MICROWAVE *1 cup* morsels, sweetened condensed milk and vanilla extract in medium, microwave-safe bowl on HIGH (100%) power for 1 minute; stir. Microwave at additional 10- to 20-second intervals, stirring until smooth. Pour evenly over crust. Top with nuts and *remaining* morsels.

BAKE for 20 to 25 minutes or until edges are bubbly. Cool completely in pan on wire rack. Cut into bars.
Makes 2 dozen bars

Rocky Road Bars

2 cups (12-ounce package) NESTLÉ TOLL HOUSE Semi-Sweet
    Chocolate Morsels, *divided*
1½ cups all-purpose flour
1½ teaspoons baking powder
  1 cup granulated sugar
  6 tablespoons (¾ stick) butter or margarine, softened
1½ teaspoons vanilla extract
  2 large eggs
  2 cups miniature marshmallows
1½ cups coarsely chopped walnuts

PREHEAT oven to 375°F. Grease 13 × 9-inch baking pan.

MICROWAVE *1 cup* morsels in medium, microwave-safe bowl on HIGH (100%)
power for 1 minute; stir. Microwave at additional 10- to 20-second intervals; stir until
smooth. Cool to room temperature. Combine flour and baking powder in small bowl.

BEAT sugar, butter and vanilla extract in large mixer bowl until crumbly. Beat in eggs.
Add melted chocolate; beat until smooth. Gradually beat in flour mixture. Spread
batter into prepared baking pan.

BAKE for 16 to 20 minutes or until wooden pick inserted in center comes out slightly
sticky.

REMOVE from oven; sprinkle immediately with marshmallows, nuts and *remaining*
morsels. Return to oven for 2 minutes or just until marshmallows begin to melt. Cool
in pan on wire rack for 20 to 30 minutes. Cut into bars with wet knife. Serve warm.

Makes 2½ dozen bars

Deluxe Toll House® Mud Bars

1 cup plus 2 tablespoons all-purpose flour
½ teaspoon baking soda
½ teaspoon salt
¾ cup packed brown sugar
½ cup (1 stick) butter, softened
1 teaspoon vanilla extract
1 large egg
2 cups (12-ounce package) NESTLÉ TOLL HOUSE Semi-Sweet
   Chocolate Morsels, *divided*
½ cup chopped walnuts

PREHEAT oven to 375°F. Grease 9-inch-square baking pan.

COMBINE flour, baking soda and salt in small bowl. Beat sugar, butter and vanilla extract in large mixer bowl until creamy. Beat in egg; gradually beat in flour mixture. Stir in *1¼ cups* morsels and nuts. Spread into prepared baking pan.

BAKE for 20 to 23 minutes. Remove pan to wire rack. Sprinkle with *remaining* morsels. Let stand for 5 minutes or until morsels are shiny; spread evenly. Cool in pan on wire rack. Cut into bars.   *Makes 3 dozen bars*

Outrageous Cookie Bars

½ cup (1 stick) butter or margarine
1½ cups graham cracker crumbs
1 can (14 ounces) NESTLÉ CARNATION Sweetened Condensed Milk
2 cups (12-ounce package) NESTLÉ TOLL HOUSE Semi-Sweet Chocolate
   Morsels
1 cup flaked coconut
1 cup chopped walnuts

PREHEAT oven to 350°F.

MELT butter in 13 × 9-inch baking pan in oven; remove from oven. Sprinkle graham cracker crumbs over butter. Stir well; press onto bottom of pan. Pour sweetened condensed milk evenly over crumbs. Sprinkle with morsels, coconut and nuts; press down firmly.

BAKE for 25 to 30 minutes or until light golden brown. Cool completely in pan on wire rack. Cut into bars.   *Makes 2 to 3 dozen bars*

Fabulous Pies & Tarts

Nestlé® Toll House® Chocolate Chip Pie

1 *unbaked* 9-inch (4-cup volume) deep-dish pie shell*
2 large eggs
½ cup all-purpose flour
½ cup granulated sugar
½ cup packed brown sugar
¾ cup (1½ sticks) butter, softened
1 cup (6 ounces) NESTLÉ TOLL HOUSE Semi-Sweet Chocolate Morsels
1 cup chopped nuts
Sweetened whipped cream or ice cream (optional)

If using frozen pie shell, use deep-dish style, thawed completely. Bake on baking sheet; increase baking time slightly.

PREHEAT oven to 325°F.

BEAT eggs in large mixer bowl on high speed until foamy. Beat in flour, granulated sugar and brown sugar. Beat in butter. Stir in morsels and nuts. Spoon into pie shell.

BAKE for 55 to 60 minutes or until knife inserted halfway between outside edge and center comes out clean. Cool on wire rack. Serve warm with whipped cream.

Makes 8 servings

Strawberry Cheesecake Pie

1 *prepared* 9-inch (6 ounces) graham cracker crumb crust
⅔ cup (5 fluid-ounce can) NESTLÉ CARNATION Evaporated Fat Free Milk
1 package (8 ounces) fat-free cream cheese, softened
1 large egg
½ cup granulated sugar
2 tablespoons all-purpose flour
1 teaspoon grated lemon peel
1½ to 2 cups halved fresh strawberries
3 tablespoons strawberry jelly, warmed

PREHEAT oven to 325°F.

PLACE evaporated milk, cream cheese, egg, sugar, flour and lemon peel in blender; cover. Blend until smooth. Pour into crust.

BAKE for 35 to 40 minutes or until center is set. Cool completely in pan on wire rack. Arrange strawberries on top of pie; drizzle with jelly. Refrigerate well before serving.

Makes 8 servings

Creamy Frozen Lime Pie

1 *prepared* 9-inch (6 ounces) graham cracker crumb crust
1 package (8 ounces) cream cheese, softened
1 can (14 ounces) NESTLÉ CARNATION Sweetened Condensed Milk
1 cup NESTLÉ CARNATION Evaporated Milk
½ cup (about 3 medium limes) lime juice
1 teaspoon grated lime peel
Lime slices, berries or mint sprigs (optional)

BEAT cream cheese in small mixer bowl until smooth. Gradually add sweetened condensed milk and evaporated milk; beat until smooth.

ADD lime juice and lime peel; beat on medium speed for 1 minute. Pour into crust; freeze for at least 2 hours or until firm.

LET stand at room temperature for 10 to 15 minutes. Garnish with lime slices, berries or mint sprigs. Serve immediately.

Makes 8 servings

Peanut Butter-Chocolate Brownie Pie

1 *prepared* 9-inch (6 ounces) chocolate crumb crust
½ cup NESTLÉ TOLL HOUSE Baking Cocoa
½ cup all-purpose flour
¼ teaspoon salt
2 large eggs
1¼ teaspoons vanilla extract, *divided*
1 cup granulated sugar
½ cup (1 stick) butter or margarine, melted
1⅔ cups (11-ounce package) NESTLÉ TOLL HOUSE Peanut Butter & Milk
    Chocolate Morsels, *divided*
⅔ cup heavy whipping cream
    Vanilla or chocolate ice cream

PREHEAT oven to 350°F.

COMBINE cocoa, flour and salt in small bowl. Beat eggs and *1 teaspoon* vanilla extract in small mixer bowl; blend in sugar and butter. Add cocoa mixture; blend well. Stir in *¾ cup* morsels. Place crust on baking sheet; pour batter into crust.

BAKE for 45 minutes or until set. Cool on wire rack.

COMBINE *remaining* morsels, cream and *remaining* vanilla extract in small, microwave-safe bowl. Microwave on MEDIUM-HIGH (70%) power for 1½ minutes; stir. Microwave at additional 10- to 20-second intervals, stirring until smooth. Cut pie into wedges; top with ice cream. Spoon sauce over ice cream. *Makes 8 servings*

Custard Tart with Fresh Berries

Crust
  2 cups graham cracker crumbs
  3 tablespoons powdered sugar
  6 tablespoons butter or margarine, melted

Filling
  2 cups sour cream
  1 can (14 ounces) NESTLÉ CARNATION Sweetened Condensed Milk
  ½ cup orange juice
  2 large eggs
  1 teaspoon vanilla extract

Glaze
  1 tablespoon water
  1 teaspoon cornstarch
  ¼ cup raspberry preserves
  1 cup fresh berries (raspberries, blueberries, blackberries and/or sliced
    strawberries)

For Crust

PREHEAT oven to 350°F.

COMBINE graham cracker crumbs and sugar in medium bowl; stir in butter. Press onto bottom and 1½ inches up side of ungreased 9-inch springform pan.

BAKE for 8 to 10 minutes.

For Filling

COMBINE sour cream, sweetened condensed milk, juice, eggs and vanilla extract in large mixer bowl; beat until smooth. Gently pour into crust.

BAKE for 35 to 40 minutes or until center is set. Cool in pan on wire rack.

For Glaze

COMBINE water and cornstarch in small saucepan; stir in preserves. Bring to a boil over medium-high heat, stirring constantly. Remove from heat; strain to remove seeds. Cool for 10 minutes. Drizzle over filling. Arrange berries on top. Cover; refrigerate. Remove side of springform pan. *Makes 8 servings*

Carnation® Key Lime Pie

1 *prepared* 9-inch (6 ounces) graham cracker crumb crust
1 can (14 ounces) NESTLÉ CARNATION Sweetened Condensed Milk
½ cup (about 3 medium limes) fresh lime juice
1 teaspoon grated lime peel
2 cups frozen whipped topping, thawed
   Lime peel twists or lime slices (optional)

BEAT sweetened condensed milk and lime juice in small mixer bowl until combined; stir in lime peel. Pour into crust; spread with whipped topping. Refrigerate for 2 hours or until set. Garnish with lime peel twists.   *Makes 8 servings*

Pumpkin Cheesecake Tarts

⅔ cup (about 15) crushed gingersnap cookies
2 tablespoons butter or margarine, melted
1 package (8 ounces) cream cheese, softened
1 cup LIBBY'S 100% Pure Pumpkin
½ cup granulated sugar
1 teaspoon pumpkin pie spice
1 teaspoon vanilla extract
2 large eggs
2 tablespoons sour cream (optional)
2 tablespoons NESTLÉ TOLL HOUSE Semi-Sweet Chocolate Morsels (optional)

PREHEAT oven to 325°F. Paper-line 12 muffin cups.

COMBINE cookie crumbs and butter in small bowl. Press scant tablespoon onto bottom of each of prepared muffin cups. Bake for 5 minutes.

BEAT cream cheese, pumpkin, sugar, pumpkin pie spice and vanilla extract in small mixer bowl until blended. Add eggs; beat well. Pour into muffin cups, filling ¾ full.

BAKE for 25 to 30 minutes. Cool in pan on wire rack. Remove tarts from pan; refrigerate. Garnish with sour cream. Place morsels in *heavy-duty* resealable plastic food storage bag. Microwave on HIGH (100%) power for 20 seconds; knead. Microwave at additional 10-second intervals, kneading until smooth. Cut tiny corner from bag; squeeze to drizzle over tarts.   *Makes 12 tarts*

Pumpkin Dutch Apple Pie

Apple Layer
- 1 *unbaked* 9-inch (4-cup volume) deep-dish pie shell with high fluted edge
- 2 cups (about 2 medium) peeled, cored and thinly sliced green apples
- ¼ cup granulated sugar
- 2 teaspoons all-purpose flour
- 1 teaspoon lemon juice
- ¼ teaspoon ground cinnamon

Pumpkin Layer
- 1½ cups LIBBY'S 100% Pure Pumpkin
- 1 cup NESTLÉ CARNATION Evaporated Milk
- ½ cup granulated sugar
- 2 large eggs, lightly beaten
- 2 tablespoons butter or margarine, melted
- ¾ teaspoon ground cinnamon
- ¼ teaspoon salt
- ⅛ teaspoon ground nutmeg
- Crumb Topping (recipe follows)

PREHEAT oven to 375°F.

For Apple Layer
COMBINE apples with sugar, flour, lemon juice and cinnamon in medium bowl; pour into pie shell.

For Pumpkin Layer
COMBINE pumpkin, evaporated milk, sugar, eggs, butter, cinnamon, salt and nutmeg in medium bowl; pour over apple mixture.

BAKE for 30 minutes. Remove from oven; sprinkle with Crumb Topping. Return to oven; bake for 20 minutes or until custard is set. Cool completely on wire rack.

Makes 8 servings

Crumb Topping
COMBINE ½ cup all-purpose flour, ⅓ cup chopped walnuts and 5 tablespoons granulated sugar in medium bowl. Cut in 3 tablespoons butter with pastry blender or two knives until mixture resembles coarse crumbs.

Sweet Potato Pies

2 *unbaked* 9-inch (2-cup volume) pie shells
2 large or 3 medium (about 1½ to 2 pounds) sweet potatoes
½ cup (1 stick) butter or margarine, softened
1 cup granulated sugar
2 tablespoons packed brown sugar
⅔ cup (5 fluid-ounce can) NESTLÉ CARNATION Evaporated Milk
2 large eggs, beaten
1 teaspoon lemon juice
1 teaspoon vanilla extract
1 teaspoon ground cinnamon
¼ teaspoon ground nutmeg
⅛ teaspoon salt

COOK sweet potatoes in boiling water for 45 to 50 minutes or until tender. Drain, cool slightly and peel.

PREHEAT oven to 425°F.

MASH warm sweet potatoes and butter in large bowl. Stir in granulated sugar, brown sugar, evaporated milk and eggs. Stir in lemon juice, vanilla extract, cinnamon, nutmeg and salt. Pour into prepared pie shells.

BAKE for 15 minutes. Reduce heat to 350°F.; bake for 30 to 40 minutes or until knife inserted near center comes out clean. Cool on wire rack for 2 hours. Serve immediately or refrigerate.

Makes 16 servings

Strawberry Almond Chocolate Tart

   1 purchased refrigerated pastry for 9-inch pie
¼ cup strawberry jam
   1 cup (6 ounces) NESTLÉ TOLL HOUSE Semi-Sweet Chocolate Morsels
⅔ cup NESTLÉ CARNATION Sweetened Condensed Milk
   1 tablespoon amaretto liqueur or ½ teaspoon almond extract
   2 cups sliced strawberries
   3 tablespoons toasted almonds

PREHEAT oven to 425°F.

PLACE unfolded pastry on ungreased baking sheet. Turn edges under ½ inch; flute. Prick pastry with tines of a fork. Bake for 10 to 12 minutes or until golden brown. Cool completely on wire rack. Spread with jam.

MICROWAVE morsels and sweetened condensed milk in medium, microwave-safe bowl on HIGH (100%) power for 1 minute; stir until smooth. Microwave a few seconds longer, if necessary. Stir in liqueur. Pour over jam; spread to edges. Refrigerate for 1 hour or until chocolate is set.

ARRANGE strawberries over chocolate; sprinkle with almonds. Serve immediately.

Makes 8 servings

tip

To toast nuts, spread them in a single layer on a baking sheet and bake in a preheated 350°F. oven for 8 to 10 minutes or until very lightly browned. Or, toast nuts in an ungreased skillet over medium heat until golden brown, stirring frequently.

Easy Coconut Banana Cream Pie

1 *prebaked* 9-inch (4-cup volume) deep-dish pie shell
1 can (14 ounces) NESTLÉ CARNATION Sweetened Condensed Milk
1 cup cold water
1 package (3.4 ounces) vanilla or banana cream instant pudding and
   pie filling mix
1 cup flaked coconut
1 container (8 ounces) frozen whipped topping, thawed, *divided*
2 medium bananas, sliced, dipped in lemon juice
   Toasted or tinted flaked coconut (optional)

COMBINE sweetened condensed milk and water in large bowl. Add pudding and coconut; mix well. Fold in *1½ cups* whipped topping.

ARRANGE single layer of bananas on bottom of pie crust. Pour filling into crust. Top with *remaining* whipped topping. Refrigerate for 4 hours or until very set. Top with toasted or tinted coconut.   *Makes 8 servings*

Note: To make 2 pies, divide filling between 2 *prebaked* 9-inch (2-cup volume *each*) pie crusts. Top with *remaining* whipped topping.

Mini Morsel Ice Cream Pie

1½ cups graham cracker crumbs
½ cup (1 stick) butter, melted
¼ cup granulated sugar
1 cup (6 ounces) NESTLÉ TOLL HOUSE Semi-Sweet Chocolate Mini Morsels
1 quart ice cream or frozen yogurt, softened

COMBINE graham cracker crumbs, butter and sugar in medium bowl; stir in morsels. Press *2½ cups* crumb mixture evenly on bottom and side of 9-inch pie plate. Freeze for 15 minutes or until firm. Spread softened ice cream evenly in pie shell. Top with *remaining* crumb mixture; freeze for 2 hours or until firm.   *Makes 8 servings*

Chocolate Truffle Tart

Crust

⅔ cup all-purpose flour
½ cup powdered sugar
½ cup ground walnuts
6 tablespoons butter or margarine, softened
⅓ cup NESTLÉ TOLL HOUSE Baking Cocoa

Filling

1¼ cups heavy whipping cream
¼ cup granulated sugar
2 cups (12-ounce package) NESTLÉ TOLL HOUSE Semi-Sweet
   Chocolate Morsels
2 tablespoons seedless raspberry jam
   Sweetened whipped cream (optional)
   Fresh raspberries (optional)

For Crust

PREHEAT oven to 350°F.

BEAT flour, powdered sugar, nuts, butter and cocoa in large mixer bowl until soft dough forms. Press dough onto bottom and up side of ungreased 9- or 9½-inch fluted tart pan with removable bottom or 9-inch pie plate.

BAKE for 12 to 14 minutes or until puffed. Cool completely in pan on wire rack.

For Filling

BRING cream and granulated sugar in medium saucepan *just to a boil,* stirring occasionally. Remove from heat. Stir in morsels and jam; let stand for 5 minutes. Whisk until smooth. Transfer to small mixer bowl. Cover; refrigerate for 45 to 60 minutes or until mixture is cooled and slightly thickened.

BEAT for 20 to 30 seconds or just until color lightens slightly. Spoon into crust. Refrigerate until firm. Remove side of pan; garnish with whipped cream and raspberries.

Makes 8 servings

Apple Butterscotch Tart

Pastry for single-crust pie
5 cups (about 5 medium) peeled and thinly sliced tart green apples
1 cup (6 ounces) NESTLÉ TOLL HOUSE Butterscotch Flavored Morsels
¾ cup all-purpose flour
½ cup packed brown sugar
½ teaspoon ground cinnamon
¼ cup (½ stick) *chilled* butter or margarine
Ice cream or sweetened whipped cream

PREHEAT oven to 375°F.

LINE 9-inch tart pan with removable bottom with pastry; trim away excess pastry. Arrange apples in pastry shell; sprinkle morsels over apples. Combine flour, sugar and cinnamon in medium bowl. Cut in butter with pastry blender or two knives until mixture resembles coarse crumbs. Sprinkle mixture over filling.

BAKE for 40 to 45 minutes or until apples are tender when pierced with a sharp knife. Remove side of tart pan. Serve warm with ice cream. *Makes 8 servings*

Mini Custard Fruit Tarts

6 *prepared* single-serving graham cracker crumb crusts
1 package (3 ounces) vanilla pudding and pie filling mix (*not* instant)
⅓ cup water
1 can (12 fluid ounces) NESTLÉ CARNATION Evaporated Lowfat Milk
1 teaspoon grated lemon peel
Sliced fresh strawberries, kiwi, blueberries, raspberries, or orange sections (optional)
Mint leaves (optional)

COMBINE pudding mix and water in small saucepan. Add evaporated milk and lemon peel; stir until smooth. Cook over medium-low heat, stirring constantly, until mixture comes to a boil and thickens.

POUR into crusts; refrigerate for 1 hour or until set. Top with fruit and mint leaves before serving. *Makes 6 servings*

Variation: For a Key Lime twist to this recipe, substitute 2 teaspoons fresh lime juice and 1 teaspoon grated lime peel for the grated lemon peel. Top with lime slice.

Walnut Crunch Pumpkin Pie

    1 *unbaked* 9-inch (4-cup volume) deep-dish pie shell
1¼ cups coarsely chopped walnuts
  ¾ cup packed brown sugar
    1 can (15 ounces) LIBBY'S 100% Pure Pumpkin
    1 can (12 fluid ounces) NESTLÉ CARNATION Evaporated Milk
  ¾ cup granulated sugar
    2 large eggs, lightly beaten
1½ teaspoons pumpkin pie spice
  ¼ teaspoon salt
    3 tablespoons butter, melted

PREHEAT oven to 425°F.

COMBINE walnuts and brown sugar in small bowl. Place *¾ cup* of nut-sugar mixture on bottom of pie shell. Combine pumpkin, evaporated milk, granulated sugar, eggs, pumpkin pie spice and salt in medium bowl; mix well. Pour batter over nuts.

BAKE for 15 minutes. Reduce temperature to 350°F.; bake for 40 to 50 minutes or until knife inserted near center comes out clean. Cool on wire rack.

COMBINE butter and *remaining* nut-sugar mixture; stir until moistened. Sprinkle over cooled pie. Broil about 5 inches from heat for 2 to 3 minutes or until bubbly. Cool before serving.   *Makes 8 servings*

Libby's® Famous Pumpkin Pie

¾ cup granulated sugar
1 teaspoon ground cinnamon
½ teaspoon salt
½ teaspoon ground ginger
¼ teaspoon ground cloves
2 large eggs
1 can (15 ounces) LIBBY'S 100% Pure Pumpkin
1 can (12 fluid ounces) NESTLÉ CARNATION Evaporated Milk
1 *unbaked* 9-inch (4-cup volume) deep-dish pie shell
  Whipped cream

MIX sugar, cinnamon, salt, ginger and cloves in small bowl. Beat eggs in large bowl. Stir in pumpkin and sugar-spice mixture. Gradually stir in evaporated milk.

POUR into pie shell.

BAKE in preheated 425°F. oven for 15 minutes. Reduce temperature to 350°F.; bake for 40 to 50 minutes or until knife inserted near center comes out clean. Cool on wire rack for 2 hours. Serve immediately or refrigerate. Top with whipped cream before serving.

Makes 8 servings

Note: Do not freeze, as this will cause the crust to separate from the filling.

Tip: 1¾ teaspoons pumpkin pie spice may be substituted for cinnamon, ginger and cloves; however, the taste will be slightly different.

For 2 shallow pies: Substitute two 9-inch (2-cup volume) pie shells. Bake in preheated 425°F. oven for 15 minutes. Reduce temperature to 350°F.; bake for 20 to 30 minutes or until pies test done.

Deep-Dish Peach Custard Pie

1 *unbaked* 9-inch (4-cup volume) deep-dish pie shell
3½ cups (about 7 medium) peeled, pitted and sliced peaches
1 can (14 ounces) NESTLÉ CARNATION Sweetened Condensed Milk
2 large eggs
¼ cup butter or margarine, melted
1 to 3 teaspoons lemon juice
½ teaspoon ground cinnamon
    Dash ground nutmeg
    Streusel Topping (recipe follows)

PREHEAT oven to 425°F.

ARRANGE peaches in pie shell. Combine sweetened condensed milk, eggs, butter, lemon juice, cinnamon and nutmeg in large mixer bowl; beat until smooth. Pour over peaches.

BAKE for 10 minutes. Sprinkle with Streusel Topping. Reduce temperature to 350°F.; bake for additional 55 to 60 minutes or until knife inserted near center comes out clean. Cool on wire rack.

Makes 8 servings

Streusel Topping
COMBINE ⅓ cup packed brown sugar, ⅓ cup all-purpose flour and ⅓ cup chopped walnuts in medium bowl. Cut in 2 tablespoons butter or margarine with pastry blender or two knives until mixture resembles coarse crumbs.

Pumpkin Cheese-Swirled Pie

1 *unbaked* 9-inch (4-cup volume) deep-dish pie shell
1 package (3 ounces) cream cheese, softened
½ cup light corn syrup, *divided*
½ teaspoon vanilla extract (optional)
1 cup LIBBY'S 100% Pure Pumpkin
½ cup NESTLÉ CARNATION Evaporated Milk
2 large eggs, lightly beaten
¼ cup granulated sugar
2 teaspoons pumpkin pie spice
¼ teaspoon salt (optional)

PREHEAT oven to 325°F.

BEAT cream cheese in small mixer bowl until light and fluffy. Gradually add *¼ cup* corn syrup and vanilla extract; beat until smooth.

COMBINE pumpkin, evaporated milk, eggs, *remaining* corn syrup, sugar, pumpkin pie spice and salt in medium bowl. Pour into pie shell. Drop cream cheese mixture by rounded tablespoon onto pumpkin filling. Swirl mixture with spoon, pulling pumpkin mixture up to surface.

BAKE for 50 to 60 minutes or until knife inserted near center comes out clean. Cool completely on wire rack.   *Makes 8 servings*

Chocolate Satin Pie

1 *prepared* 9-inch (6 ounces) graham cracker crumb crust
1 can (12 fluid ounces) NESTLÉ CARNATION Evaporated Milk
2 large egg yolks
2 cups (12-ounce package) NESTLÉ TOLL HOUSE Semi-Sweet
    Chocolate Morsels
    Whipped cream
    Chopped nuts (optional)

WHISK together evaporated milk and egg yolks in medium saucepan. Heat over medium-low heat, stirring constantly, until mixture is very hot and thickens slightly; do not boil. Remove from heat; stir in morsels until completely melted and mixture is smooth.

POUR into crust; refrigerate for 3 hours or until firm. Top with whipped cream before serving; sprinkle with nuts.

Makes 10 servings

Easy Pumpkin Cream Pie

1 *prepared* 9-inch (6 ounces) graham cracker crumb crust
1 can (15 ounces) LIBBY'S 100% Pure Pumpkin
1 package (5.1 ounces) vanilla instant pudding and pie filling mix
1 cup milk
1 teaspoon pumpkin pie spice
2 cups (about 6 ounces) frozen nondairy whipped topping, thawed, *divided*
    Fresh raspberries (optional)

COMBINE pumpkin, pudding mix, milk and pumpkin pie spice in large mixer bowl; beat for 1 minute or until blended. Fold in *1½ cups* whipped topping. Spoon into crust. Freeze for at least 4 hours or until firm. Let stand in refrigerator 1 hour before serving. Garnish with *remaining* whipped topping and raspberries. Serve immediately.

Makes 8 servings

Chocolate Mudslide Frozen Pie

1 *prepared* 9-inch (6 ounces) chocolate crumb crust
1 cup (6 ounces) NESTLÉ TOLL HOUSE Semi-Sweet Chocolate Morsels
1 teaspoon TASTER'S CHOICE 100% Pure Instant Coffee
1 teaspoon hot water
¾ cup sour cream
½ cup granulated sugar
1 teaspoon vanilla extract
1½ cups heavy whipping cream
1 cup powdered sugar
¼ cup NESTLÉ TOLL HOUSE Baking Cocoa
2 tablespoons NESTLÉ TOLL HOUSE Semi-Sweet Chocolate Mini Morsels

MELT *1 cup* morsels in small, *heavy-duty* saucepan over *lowest possible* heat. When morsels begin to melt, remove from heat; stir. Return to heat for a few seconds at a time, stirring until smooth. Remove from heat; cool for 10 minutes.

COMBINE Taster's Choice and water in medium bowl. Add sour cream, granulated sugar and vanilla extract; stir until sugar is dissolved. Stir in melted chocolate until smooth. Spread into crust; refrigerate.

BEAT cream, powdered sugar and cocoa in small mixer bowl until stiff peaks form. Spread or pipe over chocolate layer. Sprinkle with mini morsels. Freeze for at least 6 hours or until firm.

Makes 8 servings

Pumpkin Pecan Pie

Pumpkin Layer
  1 *unbaked* 9-inch (4-cup volume) deep-dish pie shell
  1 cup LIBBY'S 100% Pure Pumpkin
  ⅓ cup granulated sugar
  1 large egg
  1 teaspoon pumpkin pie spice

Pecan Layer
  ⅔ cup light corn syrup
  ½ cup granulated sugar
  2 large eggs
  3 tablespoons butter or margarine, melted
  ½ teaspoon vanilla extract
  1 cup pecan halves

PREHEAT oven to 350°F.

For Pumpkin Layer
COMBINE pumpkin, sugar, egg and pumpkin pie spice in medium bowl; stir well. Spread over bottom of pie shell.

For Pecan Layer
COMBINE corn syrup, sugar, eggs, butter and vanilla extract in same bowl; stir in nuts. Spoon over pumpkin layer.

BAKE for 50 minutes or until knife inserted in center comes out clean. Cool on wire rack.

Makes 8 servings

Mississippi Mud Pie

1 *prepared* 9-inch (6 ounces) chocolate crumb crust
1 cup powdered sugar
1 cup (6 ounces) NESTLÉ TOLL HOUSE Semi-Sweet Chocolate Morsels
¼ cup (½ stick) butter or margarine, cut up
¼ cup heavy whipping cream
2 tablespoons light corn syrup
1 teaspoon vanilla extract
¾ cup chopped nuts, *divided* (optional)
2 pints coffee ice cream, softened slightly, *divided*
  Whipped cream (optional)

HEAT sugar, morsels, butter, cream and corn syrup in small, *heavy-duty* saucepan over low heat, stirring constantly, until butter is melted and mixture is smooth. Remove from heat. Stir in vanilla extract. Cool until slightly warm.

DRIZZLE ⅓ *cup* chocolate sauce in bottom of crust; sprinkle with ¼ *cup* nuts. Layer *1 pint* ice cream, scooping thin slices with a large spoon; freeze for 1 hour. Repeat with ⅓ *cup* sauce, ¼ *cup* nuts and *remaining* ice cream. Drizzle with *remaining* sauce; top with *remaining* nuts. Freeze for 2 hours or until firm. Top with whipped cream before serving.

Makes 8 servings

No-Bake Chocolate Cheesecake Pie

1 *prepared* 9-inch (6 ounces) chocolate crumb crust
4 bars (8-ounce box) NESTLÉ TOLL HOUSE Semi-Sweet Chocolate Baking Bars,
    melted and cooled
2 packages (8 ounces *each*) cream cheese, softened
¾ cup packed brown sugar
¼ cup granulated sugar
2 tablespoons milk
1 teaspoon vanilla extract
  Sweetened whipped cream (optional)

BEAT cream cheese, brown sugar, granulated sugar, milk and vanilla extract in small mixer bowl on high speed for 2 minutes. Add melted chocolate; beat on medium speed for 2 minutes.

SPOON into crust; refrigerate for 1½ hours or until firm. Top with whipped cream.

Makes 10 servings

Cakes & Cheesecakes

Vermont Spice Cake

Cake

    3 cups all-purpose flour
3½ teaspoons baking powder
    2 teaspoons pumpkin pie spice
    1 teaspoon baking soda
    ¾ teaspoon ground nutmeg
    ½ teaspoon salt
1½ cups granulated sugar
    ¾ cup (1½ sticks) butter, softened
    3 large eggs
1½ cups LIBBY'S 100% Pure Pumpkin
    ½ cup NESTLÉ CARNATION Evaporated Milk
    ¼ cup water
1½ teaspoons vanilla extract

Maple Frosting

    11 ounces cream cheese, softened
    ⅓ cup butter, softened
3½ cups sifted powdered sugar
    2 to 3 teaspoons maple flavoring
        Orange peel twists, fresh mint, chopped nuts or nut halves (optional)

PREHEAT oven to 325°F. Grease and flour two 9-inch-round cake pans.

continued on page 98

Vermont Spice Cake, continued

For Cake

COMBINE flour, baking powder, pumpkin pie spice, baking soda, nutmeg and salt in small bowl. Beat granulated sugar and butter in large mixer bowl until creamy. Add eggs; beat for 2 minutes. Beat in pumpkin, evaporated milk, water and vanilla extract. Gradually beat in flour mixture. Spread evenly into prepared cake pans.

BAKE for 35 to 40 minutes or until wooden pick inserted in center comes out clean. Cool in pans on wire racks for 15 minutes; remove to wire racks to cool completely.

For Maple Frosting

BEAT cream cheese, butter and powdered sugar in large mixer bowl until fluffy. Add maple flavoring; mix well.

To Assemble

CUT each layer in half horizontally with long, serrated knife. Frost between layers and on top of cake, leaving side unfrosted. Garnish as desired.   *Makes 12 servings*

Note: To make a 2-layer cake, frost between layers, over top and on side of cake.

Choco-holic Cake

1 package (18.25 ounces) chocolate cake mix
1 package (3.4 ounces) chocolate instant pudding and pie filling mix
1 cup milk
½ cup sour cream
4 large eggs
2 cups (12-ounce package) NESTLÉ TOLL HOUSE Semi-Sweet
    Chocolate Morsels
1 cup chopped walnuts
    Powdered sugar
    Raspberries (optional)

PREHEAT oven to 350°F. Grease and flour 12-cup bundt pan or other round tube pan.

COMBINE cake mix, pudding mix, milk, sour cream and eggs in large mixer bowl. Beat on low speed just until blended. Beat on high speed for 2 minutes. Stir in morsels and nuts. Pour into prepared bundt pan or other tube pan.

BAKE for 55 to 65 minutes or until wooden pick inserted in cake comes out clean.

COOL in pan for 20 minutes. Invert onto wire rack to cool completely. Sprinkle with powdered sugar; garnish with raspberries.   *Makes 24 servings*

Butterscotch Pumpkin Cake

1⅔ cups (11-ounce package) NESTLÉ TOLL HOUSE Butterscotch Flavored
    Morsels, *divided*
2 cups all-purpose flour
1¾ cups granulated sugar
1 tablespoon baking powder
1½ teaspoons ground cinnamon
1 teaspoon salt
½ teaspoon ground nutmeg
1 cup LIBBY'S 100% Pure Pumpkin
½ cup vegetable oil
3 large eggs
1 teaspoon vanilla extract
Powdered sugar (optional)
Butterscotch Sauce (recipe follows)

PREHEAT oven to 350°F. Grease 12-cup bundt pan.

MICROWAVE *1 cup* morsels in small, microwave-safe bowl on MEDIUM-HIGH (70%) power for 1 minute; stir. Microwave at additional 10- to 20-second intervals, stirring until smooth. Cool to room temperature.

COMBINE flour, granulated sugar, baking powder, cinnamon, salt and nutmeg in medium bowl. Stir together melted morsels, pumpkin, vegetable oil, eggs and vanilla extract in large bowl with wire whisk. Stir in flour mixture. Spoon batter into prepared bundt pan.

BAKE for 40 to 50 minutes or until wooden pick inserted in cake comes out clean. Cool in pan on wire rack for 30 minutes; remove to wire rack to cool completely. Sprinkle with powdered sugar. Serve with Butterscotch Sauce.   *Makes 24 servings*

Butterscotch Sauce
HEAT ⅓ cup NESTLÉ CARNATION Evaporated Milk in medium, *heavy-duty* saucepan over medium heat *just to a boil;* remove from heat. Add *remaining* morsels; stir until smooth. Return to heat. Stirring constantly, bring mixture just to a boil. Cool to room temperature. Stir before serving.

Chocolate Chip Cheesecake

Crust
> 1½ cups (about 15) crushed chocolate sandwich cookies
> 2 tablespoons butter or margarine, melted
> 2 cups (12-ounce package) NESTLÉ TOLL HOUSE Semi-Sweet Chocolate Mini Morsels, *divided*

Filling
> 2 packages (8 ounces *each*) cream cheese, softened
> ½ cup granulated sugar
> 1 tablespoon vanilla extract
> 2 large eggs
> 2 tablespoons all-purpose flour
> ¾ cup NESTLÉ CARNATION Evaporated Milk
> ½ cup sour cream

For Crust
PREHEAT oven to 300°F.

COMBINE cookie crumbs with butter in medium bowl until moistened; press onto bottom of ungreased 9-inch springform pan. Sprinkle with *1 cup* morsels.

For Filling
BEAT cream cheese, sugar and vanilla extract in large mixer bowl until smooth. Beat in eggs and flour. Gradually beat in evaporated milk and sour cream. Pour over crust. Sprinkle with *remaining* morsels.

BAKE for 25 minutes. Cover loosely with aluminum foil. Bake for additional 30 to 40 minutes or until edge is set but center still moves slightly. Place in refrigerator immediately; refrigerate for 2 hours or until firm. Remove side of springform pan.

Makes 12 to 14 servings

Note: Cheesecake may be baked in 13 × 9-inch pan. Prepare as above. Bake in preheated 300°F. oven for 20 minutes. Cover loosely with aluminum foil. Bake for additional 20 to 30 minutes.

Pumpkin Pecan Rum Cake

¾ cup chopped pecans
3 cups all-purpose flour
2 tablespoons pumpkin pie spice
2 teaspoons baking soda
1 teaspoon salt
1 cup (2 sticks) butter or margarine, softened
1 cup packed brown sugar
1 cup granulated sugar
4 large eggs
1 can (15 ounces) LIBBY'S 100% Pure Pumpkin
1 teaspoon vanilla extract
Rum Butter Glaze (recipe follows)

PREHEAT oven to 325°F. Grease 12-cup bundt pan. Sprinkle nuts over bottom.

COMBINE flour, pumpkin pie spice, baking soda and salt in medium bowl. Beat butter, brown sugar and granulated sugar in large mixer bowl until light and fluffy. Add eggs; beat well. Add pumpkin and vanilla extract; beat well. Add flour mixture to pumpkin mixture, ⅓ at a time, mixing well after each addition. Spoon batter into prepared pan.

BAKE for 60 to 70 minutes or until wooden pick comes out clean. Cool 10 minutes. Make holes in cake with long pick; pour *half* of glaze over cake. Let stand 5 minutes and invert onto plate. Make holes in top of cake; pour *remaining* glaze over cake. Cool. Garnish as desired.

Makes 24 servings

Rum Butter Glaze
MELT ¼ cup butter or margarine in small saucepan; stir in ½ cup granulated sugar and 2 tablespoons water. Bring to a boil. Remove from heat; stir in 2 to 3 tablespoons dark rum or 1 teaspoon rum extract.

Chocolate Truffle Cake with Strawberry Sauce

Truffle Cake
  1¾ cups (11.5-ounce package) NESTLÉ TOLL HOUSE Milk Chocolate Morsels, *divided*
  ½ cup (1 stick) butter
  3 large eggs
  ⅔ cup granulated sugar
  1 teaspoon vanilla extract
  ¼ teaspoon salt
  ⅔ cup all-purpose flour

Glaze
  ¼ cup NESTLÉ TOLL HOUSE Butterscotch Flavored Morsels
  ¼ cup creamy peanut butter

Strawberry Sauce
  2 cups fresh or frozen strawberries, thawed
  2 tablespoons granulated sugar
  Garnish suggestions: whipped topping, fresh strawberries, fresh mint leaves

For Truffle Cake

PREHEAT oven to 350°F. Grease and flour 9-inch springform pan. Melt *1 cup* milk chocolate morsels and butter in small, microwave-safe bowl on MEDIUM-HIGH (70%) power for 1 minute; stir. Microwave at additional 10- to 20-second intervals, stirring until smooth. Cool for 10 minutes.

BEAT eggs, ⅔ cup sugar, vanilla extract and salt in large mixer bowl. Blend in chocolate mixture. Stir in flour; mix well. Pour into prepared pan.

BAKE for 30 to 35 minutes or until wooden pick inserted in center comes out clean. Cool completely in pan on wire rack. Remove side of pan.

For Glaze

MELT *remaining* milk chocolate morsels, butterscotch morsels and peanut butter in small, microwave-safe bowl on MEDIUM-HIGH (70%) power for 1 minute; stir. Microwave at additional 10- to 20-second intervals, stirring until smooth. Cool slightly. Spread glaze over top and side of cooled cake. Refrigerate for 30 minutes or until glaze is set.

For Strawberry Sauce

PLACE strawberries and 2 tablespoons sugar in blender; cover. Blend until smooth. Refrigerate until serving time. To serve, cut into wedges. Garnish with Strawberry Sauce, whipped topping, strawberries and mint leaves. *Makes 12 servings*

Cappuccino Cheesecake

1¾ cups (about 18) crushed chocolate cookies
½ cup granulated sugar, *divided*
⅓ cup butter, melted
3 packages (8 ounces *each*) cream cheese, softened
1 cup French Vanilla NESTLÉ CARNATION COFFEE-MATE Liquid
    Coffee Creamer
4 large eggs
1 tablespoon NESCAFÉ Espresso Roast
¼ cup all-purpose flour
¾ cup NESTLÉ TOLL HOUSE Premier White Morsels
2 cups (16-ounce container) sour cream, room temperature
1 bar (2 ounces *total*) NESTLÉ TOLL HOUSE Premier White Baking Bars, grated
    (optional)

PREHEAT oven to 350°F.

COMBINE cookie crumbs and ¼ *cup* sugar in small bowl; stir in butter. Press onto bottom and 1 inch up side of ungreased 9-inch springform pan. Bake for 5 minutes.

BEAT cream cheese and Coffee-Mate in large mixer bowl until creamy. Stir together eggs and Nescafé in small bowl until coffee is dissolved. Add egg mixture, flour and *remaining* sugar to cream cheese mixture; beat until combined. Spread over chocolate crust.

BAKE for additional 45 to 50 minutes or until edge is set but center still moves slightly.

MICROWAVE morsels in medium, microwave-safe bowl on MEDIUM-HIGH (70%) power for 1 minute; stir. Microwave at additional 10- to 20-second intervals, stirring until smooth. Add sour cream; stir. Spread over top of cheesecake. Bake for additional 10 minutes. Cool in pan on wire rack. Refrigerate for several hours or overnight. Garnish with grated baking bar before serving. *Makes 12 servings*

Pumpkin Cake Roll with Cream Cheese Filling

Cake

      Powdered sugar
  ¾ **cup all-purpose flour**
  ½ **teaspoon baking powder**
  ½ **teaspoon baking soda**
  ½ **teaspoon ground cinnamon**
  ½ **teaspoon ground cloves**
  ¼ **teaspoon salt**
  3 **large eggs**
  1 **cup granulated sugar**
  ⅔ **cup LIBBY'S 100% Pure Pumpkin**
  1 **cup chopped walnuts (optional)**

Filling

  1 **package (8 ounces) cream cheese, softened**
  1 **cup sifted powdered sugar**
  6 **tablespoons butter or margarine, softened**
  1 **teaspoon vanilla extract**
     Powdered sugar (optional)

For Cake

PREHEAT oven to 375°F. Grease 15 × 10-inch jelly-roll pan; line with wax paper. Grease and flour paper. Sprinkle clean towel with powdered sugar.

COMBINE flour, baking powder, baking soda, cinnamon, cloves and salt in small bowl. Beat eggs and granulated sugar in large mixer bowl until thick. Beat in pumpkin. Stir in flour mixture. Spread evenly into prepared pan. Sprinkle with nuts.

BAKE for 13 to 15 minutes or until top of cake springs back when touched. Immediately loosen and turn cake onto prepared towel. Carefully peel off paper. Roll up cake and towel together, starting with narrow end. Cool on wire rack.

For Filling

BEAT cream cheese, powdered sugar, butter and vanilla extract in small mixer bowl until smooth. Carefully unroll cake; remove towel. Spread cream cheese mixture over cake. Reroll cake. Wrap in plastic wrap and refrigerate at least one hour. Sprinkle with powdered sugar before serving.   *Makes 10 servings*

Triple Chip Cheesecake

Crust
   1¾ cups chocolate graham cracker crumbs
   ⅓ cup butter or margarine, melted

Filling
   3 packages (8 ounces *each*) cream cheese, softened
   ¾ cup granulated sugar
   ½ cup sour cream
   3 tablespoons all-purpose flour
   1½ teaspoons vanilla extract
   3 large eggs
   1 cup (6 ounces) NESTLÉ TOLL HOUSE Butterscotch Flavored Morsels
   1 cup (6 ounces) NESTLÉ TOLL HOUSE Semi-Sweet Chocolate Morsels
   1 cup (6 ounces) NESTLÉ TOLL HOUSE Premier White Morsels

Topping
   1 tablespoon *each* NESTLÉ TOLL HOUSE Butterscotch Flavored Morsels,
      Semi-Sweet Chocolate Morsels and Premier White Morsels

PREHEAT oven to 300°F. Grease 9-inch springform pan.

For Crust
COMBINE crumbs and butter in medium bowl. Press onto bottom and 1 inch up side of prepared pan.

For Filling
BEAT cream cheese and granulated sugar in large mixer bowl until smooth. Add sour cream, flour and vanilla extract; mix well. Add eggs; beat on low speed until combined. Melt butterscotch morsels according to package directions. Stir until smooth. Add *1½ cups* batter to melted morsels. Pour into crust. Repeat procedure with semi-sweet morsels. Carefully spoon over butterscotch layer. Melt Premier White morsels according to package directions and blend into *remaining* batter in mixer bowl. Carefully spoon over semi-sweet layer.

continued on page 110

Triple Chip Cheesecake, continued

BAKE for 1 hour and 10 to 15 minutes or until center is almost set. Cool in pan on wire rack for 10 minutes. Run knife around edge of cheesecake. Let stand for 1 hour.

For Topping

PLACE each flavor of morsels separately into three small, *heavy-duty* resealable plastic food storage bags. Microwave on HIGH (100%) power for 20 seconds; knead bags to mix. Microwave at additional 10-second intervals, kneading until smooth. Cut small hole in corner of each bag; squeeze to drizzle over cheesecake. Refrigerate for at least 3 hours or overnight. Remove side of pan.   *Makes 12 to 16 servings*

Marbled Chocolate Sour Cream Cake

1 cup (6 ounces) NESTLÉ TOLL HOUSE Semi-Sweet Chocolate Morsels
1 package (18.25 ounces) yellow cake mix
4 large eggs
¾ cup sour cream
½ cup vegetable oil
¼ cup water
¼ cup granulated sugar
   Powdered sugar (optional)

PREHEAT oven to 375°F. Grease 12-cup bundt or round tube pan.

MICROWAVE morsels in medium, microwave-safe bowl on HIGH (100%) power for 1 minute; stir. Microwave at additional 10- to 20-second intervals, stirring until smooth.

COMBINE cake mix, eggs, sour cream, vegetable oil, water and granulated sugar in large mixer bowl. Beat on low speed until moistened. Beat on high speed for 2 minutes.

STIR *2 cups* batter into melted chocolate. Alternately spoon batters into prepared pan, beginning and ending with yellow batter.

BAKE for 35 to 40 minutes or until wooden pick inserted in cake comes out clean. Cool in pan for 20 minutes; invert onto wire rack to cool completely. Dust with powdered sugar before serving.   *Makes 20 servings*

Apple-Scotch Snack Cake

Topping

⅔ cup quick or old-fashioned oats
6 tablespoons all-purpose flour
4 tablespoons butter, softened
3 tablespoons packed brown sugar

Cake

2¼ cups all-purpose flour
1 cup quick or old-fashioned oats
1 tablespoon baking powder
½ teaspoon salt
1 cup firmly packed brown sugar
2 large eggs
1¼ cups milk
6 tablespoons butter, melted and cooled
1 teaspoon vanilla extract
1⅓ cups peeled and finely chopped apple (about 2 small tart apples)
1⅓ cups NESTLÉ TOLL HOUSE Butterscotch Flavored Morsels, *divided*
1½ teaspoons milk
Vanilla ice cream (optional)

PREHEAT oven to 350°F. Grease bottom of 13 × 9-inch baking pan.

For Topping
COMBINE oats, flour, butter and brown sugar in small bowl. With clean fingers, mix until crumbly; set aside.

For Cake
COMBINE flour, oats, baking powder and salt in large bowl. Combine brown sugar and eggs with wire whisk. Whisk in 1¼ cups milk, melted butter and vanilla extract. Add to flour mixture all at once; add apples. Stir gently until just combined. Pour into prepared pan. Sprinkle with *1 cup* morsels; crumble topping evenly over morsels.

BAKE for 40 minutes or until golden brown and wooden pick inserted in center comes out with a few moist crumbs clinging to it. Remove from oven to wire rack. Microwave *remaining ⅓ cup* morsels and 1½ teaspoons milk in small, microwave-safe bowl. Microwave on HIGH (100% power) for 20 seconds; stir until smooth. Carefully drizzle over hot cake in pan. Cool in pan at least 30 minutes. Cut into squares; serve warm or at room temperature with ice cream. Store tightly covered at room temperature.

Makes 16 servings

Chocolate Intensity

Cake

    4 bars (8-ounce box) NESTLÉ TOLL HOUSE Unsweetened Chocolate
        Baking Bars, broken into pieces
    ½ cup (1 stick) butter, softened
  1½ cups granulated sugar
    3 large eggs
    2 teaspoons vanilla extract
    ⅔ cup all-purpose flour
      Powdered sugar (optional)

Coffee Crème Anglaise Sauce

    4 large egg yolks, lightly beaten
    ⅓ cup granulated sugar
    1 tablespoon TASTER'S CHOICE 100% Pure Instant Coffee
  1½ cups milk
    1 teaspoon vanilla extract

PREHEAT oven to 350°F. Grease 9-inch springform pan.

For Cake

MICROWAVE baking bars in medium, microwave-safe bowl on HIGH (100%) power for 1 minute; stir. Microwave at additional 10- to 20-second intervals, stirring until smooth; cool to lukewarm.

BEAT butter, granulated sugar, eggs and vanilla extract in small mixer bowl for about 4 minutes or until thick and pale yellow. Beat in melted chocolate. Gradually beat in flour. Spread into prepared springform pan.

BAKE for 25 to 28 minutes or until wooden pick inserted in center comes out moist. Cool in pan on wire rack for 15 minutes. Loosen and remove side of pan; cool completely. Sprinkle with powdered sugar; serve with Coffee Crème Anglaise Sauce.

For Coffee Crème Anglaise Sauce

PLACE egg yolks in medium bowl. Combine granulated sugar and Taster's Choice in medium saucepan; stir in milk. Cook over medium heat, stirring constantly, until mixture comes just to a very gentle boil. Remove from heat. Gradually whisk *half* of hot milk mixture into egg yolks; return mixture to saucepan. Cook, stirring constantly, for 3 to 4 minutes or until mixture is slightly thickened. Strain into small bowl; stir in vanilla extract. Cover; refrigerate.

Makes 10 to 12 servings

Pumpkin Cheesecake

Crust
 1½ cups graham cracker crumbs
 ⅓ cup butter or margarine, melted
 ¼ cup granulated sugar

Filling
 3 packages (8 ounces *each*) cream cheese, softened
 1 cup granulated sugar
 ¼ cup packed light brown sugar
 2 large eggs
 1 can (15 ounces) LIBBY'S 100% Pure Pumpkin
 ⅔ cup (5 fluid-ounce can) NESTLÉ CARNATION Evaporated Milk
 2 tablespoons cornstarch
 1¼ teaspoons ground cinnamon
 ½ teaspoon ground nutmeg

Topping
 1 container (16 ounces) sour cream, at room temperature
 ⅓ cup granulated sugar
 1 teaspoon vanilla extract

PREHEAT oven to 350°F.

For Crust
COMBINE graham cracker crumbs, butter and granulated sugar in medium bowl. Press onto bottom and 1 inch up side of 9-inch springform pan. Bake for 6 to 8 minutes (do not allow to brown). Cool on wire rack for 10 minutes.

For Filling
BEAT cream cheese, granulated sugar and brown sugar in large mixer bowl until fluffy. Beat in eggs, pumpkin and evaporated milk. Add cornstarch, cinnamon and nutmeg; beat well. Pour into crust.

BAKE for 55 to 60 minutes or until edge is set but center still moves slightly.

For Topping
MIX sour cream, granulated sugar and vanilla extract in small bowl; mix well. Spread over surface of warm cheesecake. Bake for 5 minutes. Cool on wire rack. Refrigerate for several hours or overnight. Remove side of springform pan.   *Makes 16 servings*

Bittersweet Chocolate Pound Cake

Cake

> 2 cups all-purpose flour
> 1 teaspoon baking soda
> 1 teaspoon baking powder
> 1½ cups water
> 2 tablespoons TASTER'S CHOICE 100% Pure Instant Coffee
> 3 bars (6 ounces *total*) NESTLÉ TOLL HOUSE Unsweetened Chocolate
>   Baking Bars, broken into pieces
> 2 cups granulated sugar
> 1 cup (2 sticks) butter, softened
> 1 teaspoon vanilla extract
> 3 large eggs

Chocolate Glaze

> 1 bar (2 ounces) NESTLÉ TOLL HOUSE Unsweetened Chocolate Baking Bars
> 3 tablespoons butter or margarine
> 1½ cups sifted powdered sugar
> 2 to 3 tablespoons water
> 1 teaspoon vanilla extract
>   Powdered sugar (optional)

PREHEAT oven to 325°F. Grease 12-cup bundt pan.

For Cake
COMBINE flour, baking soda and baking powder in small bowl. Bring water and Taster's Choice to a boil in small saucepan; remove from heat. Add 3 bars (6 ounces *total*) baking chocolate; stir until smooth.

BEAT granulated sugar, butter and vanilla extract in large mixer bowl until creamy. Add eggs; beat on high speed for 5 minutes. Beat in flour mixture alternately with chocolate mixture. Pour into prepared bundt pan.

BAKE for 50 to 60 minutes or until wooden pick inserted in cake comes out clean. Cool in pan on wire rack for 30 minutes. Invert onto wire rack to cool completely. Drizzle with Chocolate Glaze; sprinkle with powdered sugar.

For Chocolate Glaze
MELT baking bar and butter in small, *heavy-duty* saucepan over low heat, stirring until smooth. Remove from heat. Stir in powdered sugar alternately with water until of desired consistency. Stir in vanilla extract. *Makes 12 servings*

Spicy Chocolate Cake

Cake

1 cup (6 ounces) NESTLÉ TOLL HOUSE Semi-Sweet Chocolate Morsels
1¼ cups granulated sugar
¾ cup (1½ sticks) butter or margarine, softened
1 teaspoon vanilla extract
3 large eggs
2 cups all-purpose flour
1 tablespoon ground cinnamon
1 teaspoon baking soda
½ teaspoon salt
1 cup milk
1 to 2 tablespoons diced jalapeños (optional)

Frosting

3 to 3¼ cups sifted powdered sugar
⅓ cup milk
¼ cup (½ stick) butter or margarine, softened
2 packets (1 ounce *each*) NESTLÉ TOLL HOUSE CHOCO BAKE Unsweetened
   Chocolate Flavor
2 teaspoons vanilla extract
¼ teaspoon salt

For Cake

PREHEAT oven to 350°F. Grease two 9-inch-round cake pans or one 13 × 9-inch baking pan.

MICROWAVE morsels in medium, microwave-safe bowl on HIGH (100%) power for 1 minute, stir. Microwave at additional 10- to 20-second intervals, stirring until smooth. Let cool to room temperature.

BEAT granulated sugar, butter and vanilla extract in large mixer bowl until creamy. Add eggs; beat for 1 minute. Beat in melted chocolate. Combine flour, cinnamon, baking soda and salt in medium bowl; beat into chocolate mixture alternately with milk. Stir in jalapeños. Pour into prepared pan(s).

BAKE for 30 to 35 minutes or until wooden pick inserted in center comes out clean. Cool in pan(s) for 20 minutes; invert onto wire rack(s) to cool completely.

For Frosting

BEAT powdered sugar, milk, butter, Choco Bake, vanilla extract and salt in small mixer bowl until mixture is smooth and creamy. Frost cake.

Makes 10 to 12 servings

Premier White Lemony Cheesecake

Crust

> 6 tablespoons butter or margarine, softened
> ¼ cup granulated sugar
> 1¼ cups all-purpose flour
> 1 large egg yolk
> ⅛ teaspoon salt

Filling

> 6 bars (*two* 6-ounce boxes) NESTLÉ TOLL HOUSE Premier White Baking Bars,
>   broken into pieces or 2 cups (12-ounce package) NESTLÉ TOLL HOUSE
>   Premier White Morsels
> ½ cup heavy whipping cream
> 2 packages (8 ounces *each*) cream cheese, softened
> 1 tablespoon lemon juice
> 2 teaspoons grated lemon peel
> ¼ teaspoon salt
> 3 large egg whites
> 1 large egg

PREHEAT oven to 350°F. Lightly grease 9-inch springform pan.

For Crust

BEAT butter and sugar in small mixer bowl until creamy. Beat in flour, egg yolk and salt. Press mixture onto bottom and 1 inch up side of prepared pan.

BAKE for 14 to 16 minutes or until crust is set.

For Filling

MICROWAVE baking bars and whipping cream in medium, microwave-safe bowl on MEDIUM-HIGH (70%) power for 1 minute; stir. Microwave at additional 10- to 20-second intervals, stirring until smooth.

BEAT cream cheese, lemon juice, lemon peel and salt in large mixer bowl until smooth. Gradually beat in melted baking bars. Beat in egg whites and egg. Pour into crust.

BAKE for 35 to 40 minutes or until edge is lightly browned. Run knife around edge of cheesecake. Cool completely in pan on wire rack. Refrigerate for several hours or overnight. Remove side of springform pan. Garnish as desired.

Makes 12 to 16 servings

Brown-Eyed Susan Sweet Potato Cake

Cake

2¼ cups all-purpose flour
 1 tablespoon baking powder
 1 teaspoon baking soda
 1 teaspoon salt
 1 teaspoon ground cinnamon
 ½ teaspoon ground ginger
 1 can (15 ounces) mashed sweet potatoes or 1 can (15 ounces) unsweetened
   sweet potatoes, rinsed, drained and mashed
 1 cup granulated sugar
 ½ cup packed dark brown sugar
 3 large eggs
 1 cup vegetable oil
 1 cup (6 ounces) NESTLÉ TOLL HOUSE Semi-Sweet Chocolate Morsels
 ½ cup chopped pecans
 ½ cup water

Creamy Premier White Icing

 ¾ cup NESTLÉ TOLL HOUSE Premier White Morsels
1½ tablespoons butter or margarine
 ½ cup (4 ounces) cream cheese, softened
 ⅓ cup sour cream
 ¾ teaspoon vanilla extract
 ¼ teaspoon almond extract (optional)
 3 to 4 cups powdered sugar

For Cake

PREHEAT oven to 350°F. Lightly grease and flour two 9-inch-round cake pans or one 13 × 9-inch baking pan.

COMBINE flour, baking powder, baking soda, salt, cinnamon and ginger in small bowl. Combine sweet potatoes, granulated sugar and brown sugar in large bowl. Add eggs, one at a time, beating well after each addition. Add oil; beat until well blended. Stir in morsels, pecans and water. Stir in flour mixture; mix until blended. Pour into prepared pan(s).

BAKE for 35 to 40 minutes or until wooden pick inserted in center comes out clean. Cool completely in pan(s) on wire rack(s). For layer cakes, remove from pans after 10 minutes. Frost with Creamy Premier White Icing.

continued on page 122

Brown-Eyed Susan Sweet Potato Cake, continued

For Creamy Premier White Icing

MICROWAVE morsels and butter in small, microwave-safe mixer bowl on MEDIUM-HIGH (70%) power for 1 minute; stir. Microwave at additional 10- to 20-second intervals, stirring until smooth. Cool to room temperature.

BEAT cream cheese and sour cream into morsel mixture until creamy. Add vanilla extract and almond extract. Gradually beat in powdered sugar until mixture reaches spreading consistency. Makes about 3 cups.   *Makes 12 servings*

Tropical Sunshine Cake

    1 package (18.25 ounces) yellow cake mix
    1 can (12 fluid ounces) NESTLÉ CARNATION Evaporated Milk
    2 large eggs
    1 can (20 ounces) crushed pineapple in juice, drained (juice reserved), *divided*
    ½ cup chopped almonds
    ¾ cup sifted powdered sugar
    1 cup flaked coconut, toasted
      Whipped cream

PREHEAT oven to 350°F. Grease 13 × 9-inch baking pan.

COMBINE cake mix, evaporated milk and eggs in large mixer bowl. Beat on low speed for 2 minutes. Stir in *1 cup* pineapple. Pour batter into prepared baking pan. Sprinkle with almonds.

BAKE for 30 to 35 minutes or until wooden pick inserted in center comes out clean. Cool in pan on wire rack for 15 minutes.

COMBINE sugar and 2 tablespoons *reserved* pineapple juice in small bowl; mix until smooth. Spread over warm cake, sprinkle with coconut and *remaining* pineapple. Cool completely before serving. Top with whipped cream.   *Makes 12 servings*

Tuxedo Cheesecake

Crust

1¾ cups (about 18) crushed creme-filled chocolate cookies
2 tablespoons butter or margarine, melted

Filling

1 cup (6 ounces) NESTLÉ TOLL HOUSE Premier White Morsels
3 packages (8 ounces *each*) cream cheese, softened
¾ cup granulated sugar
2 teaspoons vanilla extract
3 large eggs
1 bar (2 ounces *total*) NESTLÉ TOLL HOUSE Semi-Sweet Chocolate or Premier White Chocolate Baking Bars, made into curls or grated

PREHEAT oven to 350°F.

For Crust

COMBINE cookie crumbs and butter together in medium bowl. Press onto bottom of ungreased 9-inch springform pan. Bake for 10 minutes.

For Filling

MICROWAVE morsels in small, microwave-safe bowl on MEDIUM-HIGH (70%) power for 1 minute; stir. Microwave at additional 10- to 20-second intervals, stirring until smooth; cool to room temperature.

BEAT cream cheese, sugar and vanilla extract in large mixer bowl until smooth. Beat in eggs; gradually beat in melted white morsels. Spread over chocolate crust.

BAKE for 40 to 50 minutes or until edge is set but center still moves slightly. Cool in pan on wire rack; refrigerate until firm. Remove side of springform pan.

SPRINKLE chocolate curls over cheesecake before serving.

Makes 14 to 16 servings

Pumpkin Carrot Cake

      2 cups all-purpose flour
      2 teaspoons baking soda
      2 teaspoons ground cinnamon
      ½ teaspoon salt
      ¾ cup milk
   1½ teaspoons lemon juice
      3 large eggs
   1¼ cups LIBBY'S 100% Pure Pumpkin
   1½ cups granulated sugar
      ½ cup packed brown sugar
      ½ cup vegetable oil
      1 can (8 ounces) crushed pineapple, drained
      1 cup (about 3 medium) grated carrots
      1 cup flaked coconut
   1¼ cups chopped nuts, *divided*
         Cream Cheese Frosting (recipe follows)

PREHEAT oven to 350°F. Grease two 9-inch-round baking pans.

COMBINE flour, baking soda, cinnamon and salt in small bowl. Combine milk and lemon juice in liquid measuring cup (mixture will appear curdled).

BEAT eggs, pumpkin, granulated sugar, brown sugar, oil, pineapple, carrots and milk mixture in large mixer bowl; mix well. Gradually add flour mixture; beat until combined. Stir in coconut and *1 cup* nuts. Pour into prepared baking pans.

BAKE for 30 to 35 minutes or until wooden pick inserted in center comes out clean. Cool in pans for 15 minutes. Remove to wire racks to cool completely.

FROST between layers, on side and top of cake with Cream Cheese Frosting. Garnish with *remaining* nuts. Store in refrigerator.   *Makes 12 servings*

Cream Cheese Frosting
COMBINE 11 ounces softened cream cheese, ⅓ cup softened butter and 3½ cups sifted powdered sugar in large mixer bowl until fluffy. Add 1 teaspoon vanilla extract, 2 teaspoons orange juice and 1 teaspoon grated orange peel; beat until combined.

Rich Chocolate Cake with Creamy Peanut Butter Milk Chocolate Frosting

Cake

   2 cups all-purpose flour
1¾ cups granulated sugar
   ⅔ cup NESTLÉ TOLL HOUSE Baking Cocoa
1½ teaspoons baking powder
1½ teaspoons baking soda
   ½ teaspoon salt
   1 cup milk
   1 cup water
   ½ cup vegetable oil
   2 large eggs
   2 teaspoons vanilla extract
1⅔ cups (11-ounce package) NESTLÉ TOLL HOUSE Peanut Butter & Milk
     Chocolate Morsels, *divided*

Creamy Peanut Butter Milk Chocolate Frosting

   1 package (8 ounces) cream cheese, softened
   1 teaspoon vanilla extract
   ⅛ teaspoon salt
   3 cups powdered sugar

Garnish

   1 bar (2 ounces *total*) NESTLÉ TOLL HOUSE Semi-Sweet Chocolate
     Baking Bars, made into curls (see Tip)

For Cake

PREHEAT oven to 350°F. Grease and flour two 9-inch-round cake pans.

COMBINE flour, granulated sugar, cocoa, baking powder, baking soda and salt in large mixer bowl. Add milk, water, vegetable oil, eggs and vanilla extract; blend until moistened. Beat for 2 minutes (batter will be thin). Pour into prepared pans. Sprinkle *⅓ cup* morsels over each cake layer.

BAKE for 25 to 30 minutes or until wooden pick inserted in center comes out clean. Cool in pans on wire racks for 10 minutes; remove to wire racks to cool completely. Frost with Creamy Peanut Butter Milk Chocolate Frosting between layers and on top and side of cake. Garnish with chocolate curls before serving.

continued on page 128

Rich Chocolate Cake with Creamy Milk Chocolate Peanut Butter Frosting,
continued

For Creamy Peanut Butter Milk Chocolate Frosting
MICROWAVE *remaining* morsels in small, microwave-safe bowl on MEDIUM-HIGH (70%) power for 1 minute; stir. Microwave at additional 10- to 20-second intervals, stirring until smooth. Beat cream cheese, melted morsels, vanilla extract and salt in small mixer bowl until light and fluffy. Gradually beat in powdered sugar.

Makes 10 to 12 servings

Tip: To make chocolate curls, carefully draw a vegetable peeler across a bar of NESTLÉ TOLL HOUSE Semi-Sweet Chocolate. Vary the width of your curls by using different sides of the chocolate bar.

White Chip Pumpkin Spice Cake

1 package (18.25 ounces) spice cake mix
3 large eggs
1 cup LIBBY'S 100% Pure Pumpkin
⅔ cup (5 fluid-ounce can) NESTLÉ CARNATION Evaporated Milk
⅓ cup vegetable oil
1 cup (6 ounces) NESTLÉ TOLL HOUSE Premier White Morsels
    White Chip Cinnamon Glaze (recipe follows)

PREHEAT oven to 350°F. Grease and flour 12-cup bundt pan.

COMBINE cake mix, eggs, pumpkin, evaporated milk and vegetable oil in large mixer bowl. Beat at low speed until moistened. Beat at medium speed for 2 minutes; stir in morsels. Pour into prepared bundt pan.

BAKE for 40 to 45 minutes or until wooden pick inserted in cake comes out clean. Cool in pan on wire rack for 25 minutes; invert onto wire rack to cool completely. Drizzle *half* of glaze over cake; serve with *remaining* glaze.   *Makes 16 servings*

White Chip Cinnamon Glaze
HEAT 3 tablespoons NESTLÉ CARNATION Evaporated Milk in small, *heavy-duty* saucepan over medium heat just to a boil; remove from heat. Add 1 cup (6 ounces) NESTLÉ TOLL HOUSE Premier White Morsels; stir until smooth. Stir in ½ teaspoon ground cinnamon.

Turtle Cheesecake

Crust
  1¾ cups chocolate graham cracker crumbs
  ⅓ cup butter or margarine, melted

Filling
   3 packages (8 ounces *each*) cream cheese, softened
   1 can (14 ounces) NESTLÉ CARNATION Sweetened Condensed Milk
   ½ cup granulated sugar
   3 large eggs
   3 tablespoons lime juice
   1 tablespoon vanilla extract
  1½ cups (9 ounces) NESTLÉ TOLL HOUSE Semi-Sweet Chocolate Morsels
   2 tablespoons Chocolate Flavor NESTLÉ NESQUIK Syrup
   2 tablespoons caramel syrup or ice cream topping
   ½ cup coarsely chopped pecans
   ¼ cup NESTLÉ TOLL HOUSE Semi-Sweet Chocolate Mini Morsels

PREHEAT oven to 300°F. Grease 9-inch springform pan.

For Crust
COMBINE crumbs and butter in medium bowl. Press onto bottom and 1 inch up side of prepared pan.

For Filling
BEAT cream cheese and sweetened condensed milk in large mixer bowl until smooth. Add sugar, eggs, lime juice and vanilla extract; beat until combined. Microwave morsels in medium, microwave-safe bowl on HIGH (100%) power for 1 minute; stir. Microwave at additional 10- to 15-second intervals, stirring just until morsels are melted. Stir *2 cups* of cheesecake batter into melted morsels; mix well. Alternately spoon batters into crust, beginning and ending with yellow batter.

BAKE for 1 hour 10 to 15 minutes or until edge is set and center moves slightly. Cool in pan on wire rack for 10 minutes; run knife around edge of cheesecake. Cool completely. Drizzle Nesquik and caramel syrup over cheesecake. Sprinkle with pecans and mini morsels. Refrigerate for several hours or overnight. Remove side of pan.

Makes 12 to 16 servings

Zesty Lemon Pound Cake

1 cup (6 ounces) NESTLÉ TOLL HOUSE Premier White Morsels or 3 bars
    (6-ounce box) NESTLÉ TOLL HOUSE Premier White Baking Bars,
    broken into pieces
2½ cups all-purpose flour
1 teaspoon baking powder
½ teaspoon salt
1 cup (2 sticks) butter, softened
1½ cups granulated sugar
2 teaspoons vanilla extract
3 large eggs
3 to 4 tablespoons (about 3 medium lemons) grated lemon peel
1⅓ cups buttermilk
1 cup powdered sugar
3 tablespoons fresh lemon juice

PREHEAT oven to 350°F. Grease and flour 12-cup bundt pan.

MELT morsels in medium, microwave-safe bowl on MEDIUM-HIGH (70%) power
for 1 minute; stir. Microwave at additional 10- to 20-second intervals, stirring until
smooth; cool slightly.

COMBINE flour, baking powder and salt in small bowl. Beat butter, granulated sugar
and vanilla extract in large mixer bowl until creamy. Beat in eggs, one at a time,
beating well after each addition. Beat in lemon peel and melted morsels. Gradually
beat in flour mixture alternately with buttermilk. Pour into prepared bundt pan.

BAKE for 50 to 55 minutes or until wooden pick inserted in cake comes out clean.
Cool in pan on wire rack for 10 minutes. Combine powdered sugar and lemon juice in
small bowl. Make holes in cake with wooden pick; pour *half* of lemon glaze over cake.
Let stand for 5 minutes. Invert onto plate. Make holes in top of cake; pour *remaining*
glaze over cake. Cool completely before serving.   *Makes 16 servings*

Mocha Dream Cake

1½ cups hot water
1 tablespoon TASTER'S CHOICE 100% Pure Instant Coffee
1 cup NESTLÉ CARNATION COFFEE-MATE Powdered Coffee Creamer
2⅓ cups all-purpose flour, *divided*
1½ teaspoons baking soda
1⅓ cups (8 ounces) NESTLÉ TOLL HOUSE Premier White Morsels
⅓ cup vegetable oil
1⅔ cups granulated sugar
4 large eggs
⅔ cup (5 fluid-ounce can) NESTLÉ CARNATION Evaporated Milk
2 tablespoons white vinegar
1 teaspoon vanilla extract
⅔ cup NESTLÉ TOLL HOUSE Baking Cocoa
Mocha Frosting (recipe follows)

PREHEAT oven to 350°F. Grease and flour two 9-inch-round cake pans.

COMBINE water and Taster's Choice in medium bowl. Stir in Coffee-Mate with wire whisk. Combine *1⅔ cups* flour and baking soda in another medium bowl. Microwave 1⅓ cups morsels and vegetable oil in large, microwave-safe bowl on MEDIUM-HIGH (70%) power for 1 minute; stir. Microwave at additional 10- to 15-second intervals, stirring just until melted. Add coffee mixture, granulated sugar, eggs, evaporated milk, vinegar and vanilla extract to melted morsels; mix with wire whisk. Gradually beat in flour mixture until combined. (Batter will be thin.) Pour *3¼ cups* batter into medium bowl; stir in *remaining* flour. Pour into prepared pans.

BLEND cocoa into *remaining* batter with wire whisk until blended. Slowly pour half of cocoa batter into center of each pan. (Batter will spread evenly outward from center.)

BAKE for 40 to 45 minutes or until wooden pick inserted in center comes out clean. Cool in pans on wire racks for 10 minutes; cool completely on wire racks. Frost cake with frosting between layers and on top and side of cake.   *Makes 10 to 12 servings*

Mocha Frosting
MICROWAVE ⅔ cup NESTLÉ TOLL HOUSE Premier White Morsels and ⅓ cup butter or margarine in microwave-safe bowl on MEDIUM-HIGH (70%) power for 1 minute; stir. Microwave at additional 10- to 15-second intervals, stirring just until melted. Combine 1 tablespoon TASTER'S CHOICE 100% Pure Instant Coffee and 1½ teaspoons water. Beat 2 packages (3 ounces *each*) softened cream cheese and coffee mixture into melted morsels. Gradually beat in 4 to 4½ cups powdered sugar until mixture reaches spreading consistency. Makes about 2½ cups.

Classic Candies

Holiday Peppermint Bark

2 cups (12-ounce package) NESTLÉ TOLL HOUSE Premier White Morsels
24 hard peppermint candies, unwrapped

LINE baking sheet with wax paper.

MICROWAVE morsels in medium, microwave-safe bowl on MEDIUM-HIGH (70%) power for 1 minute; stir. Microwave at additional 10- to 20-second intervals, stirring until smooth.

PLACE peppermint candies in *heavy-duty* resealable plastic food storage bag. Crush candies using rolling pin or other heavy object. While holding strainer over melted morsels, pour crushed candy into strainer. Shake to release all small candy pieces; reserve larger candy pieces. Stir morsel-peppermint mixture.

SPREAD mixture to desired thickness on prepared baking sheet. Sprinkle with reserved candy pieces; press in lightly. Let stand for about 1 hour or until firm. Break into pieces. Store in airtight container at room temperature.

Makes about 1 pound candy

Toll House® Famous Fudge

1½ cups granulated sugar

⅔ cup (5 fluid-ounce can) NESTLÉ CARNATION Evaporated Milk

2 tablespoons butter or margarine

¼ teaspoon salt

2 cups miniature marshmallows

1½ cups (9 ounces) NESTLÉ TOLL HOUSE Semi-Sweet Chocolate Morsels

½ cup chopped pecans or walnuts (optional)

1 teaspoon vanilla extract

LINE 8-inch-square baking pan with foil.

COMBINE sugar, evaporated milk, butter and salt in medium, *heavy-duty* saucepan. Bring to a *full rolling boil* over medium heat, stirring constantly. Boil, stirring constantly, for 4 to 5 minutes. Remove from heat.

STIR in marshmallows, morsels, nuts and vanilla extract. Stir vigorously for 1 minute or until marshmallows are melted. Pour into prepared baking pan; refrigerate for 2 hours or until firm. Lift from pan; remove foil. Cut into pieces.   *Makes 49 pieces*

For Milk Chocolate Fudge
SUBSTITUTE 1¾ cups (11.5-ounce package) NESTLÉ TOLL HOUSE Milk Chocolate Morsels for Semi-Sweet Morsels.

For Butterscotch Fudge
SUBSTITUTE 1⅔ cups (11-ounce package) NESTLÉ TOLL HOUSE Butterscotch Flavored Morsels for Semi-Sweet Morsels.

For Peanutty Chocolate Fudge
SUBSTITUTE 1⅔ cups (11-ounce package) NESTLÉ TOLL HOUSE Peanut Butter & Milk Chocolate Morsels for Semi-Sweet Morsels and ½ cup chopped peanuts for pecans or walnuts.

Easy Toffee Candy

1¼ cups (2½ sticks) butter, *divided*
35 to 40 soda crackers
1 cup packed dark brown sugar
1 can (14 ounces) NESTLÉ CARNATION Sweetened Condensed Milk
1½ cups (9 ounces) NESTLÉ TOLL HOUSE Semi-Sweet Chocolate Morsels
¾ cup finely chopped walnuts

PREHEAT oven to 425°F. Line 15 × 10-inch jelly-roll pan with *heavy-duty* foil.

MELT ¼ *cup* (½ *stick*) butter in medium saucepan. Pour into prepared jelly-roll pan. Arrange crackers over butter, breaking crackers to fit empty spaces.

MELT *remaining* butter in same saucepan; add sugar. Bring to a boil over medium heat. Reduce heat to low; cook, stirring occasionally, for 2 minutes. Remove from heat; stir in sweetened condensed milk. Pour over crackers.

BAKE for 10 to 12 minutes or until mixture is bubbly and slightly darkened. Remove from oven; cool for 1 minute.

SPRINKLE with morsels. Let stand for 5 minutes or until morsels are shiny and soft; spread evenly. Sprinkle with nuts; press into chocolate. Cool in pan on wire rack for 30 minutes. Refrigerate for about 30 minutes or until chocolate is set. Remove foil; cut into pieces.   *Makes about 50 pieces*

Milk Chocolate Almond Brickle

1¼ cups almonds, toasted and coarsely chopped
1 cup (2 sticks) butter
1½ cups packed brown sugar
1¾ cups (11.5-ounce package) NESTLÉ TOLL HOUSE Milk Chocolate Morsels

SPRINKLE nuts over bottom of well-greased 13 × 9-inch baking pan.

MELT butter in medium, *heavy-duty* saucepan over medium heat. Stir in sugar. Bring to a boil, stirring constantly. Boil, stirring constantly, for 7 minutes. Pour hot mixture over nuts; let stand for 5 minutes. Sprinkle with morsels. Let stand for 5 minutes or until morsels are shiny and soft; spread evenly.

REFRIGERATE for about 20 minutes. Break into bite-size pieces.

Makes about 50 pieces

Toasted Almond Truffles

½ cup NESTLÉ CARNATION Evaporated Milk
¼ cup granulated sugar
1¾ cups (11.5-ounce package) NESTLÉ TOLL HOUSE Milk Chocolate Morsels
½ to 1 teaspoon almond or vanilla extract
1 cup sliced almonds, finely chopped, toasted

COMBINE evaporated milk and sugar in small, *heavy-duty* saucepan. Bring to a *full rolling boil* over medium-low heat, stirring constantly. Boil, stirring constantly, for 3 minutes. Remove from heat.

STIR in morsels. Stir vigorously until mixture is smooth. Stir in almond extract. Refrigerate for 1½ to 2 hours. Shape into 1-inch balls; roll in nuts. Cover; refrigerate until ready to serve.   *Makes about 2 dozen truffles*

Chocolate Chip Cookie Brittle

1 cup (2 sticks) butter or margarine, softened
1 cup granulated sugar
1½ teaspoons vanilla extract
1 teaspoon salt
2 cups all-purpose flour
2 cups (12-ounce package) NESTLÉ TOLL HOUSE Semi-Sweet Chocolate
    Morsels, *divided*
1 cup chopped nuts

PREHEAT oven to 375°F.

BEAT butter, sugar, vanilla extract and salt in large mixer bowl. Gradually beat in flour. Stir in *1½ cups* morsels and nuts. Press into ungreased 15 × 10-inch jelly-roll pan.

BAKE for 20 to 25 minutes or until golden brown and set. Cool until just slightly warm.

MICROWAVE *remaining* morsels in small, *heavy-duty* resealable plastic food storage bag on HIGH (100%) power for 30 to 45 seconds; knead. Microwave at additional 10- to 20-second intervals, kneading until smooth. Cut tiny corner from bag; squeeze to drizzle over cookie. Allow chocolate to cool and set; break cookies into irregular pieces.   *Makes about 50 pieces*

Note: Omitting nuts could cause cookie to become dry.

Chocolate Mint Truffles

1¾ cups (11.5-ounce package) NESTLÉ TOLL HOUSE Milk Chocolate Morsels
1 cup (6 ounces) NESTLÉ TOLL HOUSE Semi-Sweet Chocolate Morsels
¾ cup heavy whipping cream
1 tablespoon peppermint extract
1½ cups finely chopped walnuts, toasted or ¼ cup NESTLÉ TOLL HOUSE Baking
  Cocoa

LINE baking sheet with wax paper.

PLACE milk chocolate and semi-sweet morsels in large mixer bowl. Heat cream to a gentle boil in small saucepan; pour over morsels. Let stand for 1 minute; stir until smooth. Stir in peppermint extract. Cover with plastic wrap; refrigerate for 35 to 45 minutes or until slightly thickened. Stir just until color lightens slightly. (*Do not overmix* or truffles will be grainy.)

DROP by rounded teaspoonful onto prepared baking sheet; refrigerate for 10 to 15 minutes. Shape into balls; roll in walnuts or cocoa. Store in airtight container in refrigerator.   *Makes about 4 dozen truffles*

Variation: After rolling chocolate mixture into balls, freeze for 30 to 40 minutes. Microwave 1¾ cups (11.5-ounce package) NESTLÉ TOLL HOUSE Milk Chocolate Morsels and 3 tablespoons vegetable shortening in medium, microwave-safe bowl on MEDIUM-HIGH (70%) power for 1 minute; stir. Microwave at additional 10- to 20-second intervals, stirring until smooth. Dip truffles into chocolate mixture; shake off excess. Place on foil-lined baking sheets. Refrigerate for 15 to 20 minutes or until set. Store in airtight container in refrigerator.

Nutty Nougat Caramel Bites

Cookie Base
2¼ cups all-purpose flour
1 teaspoon baking soda
1 teaspoon salt
1 cup (2 sticks) butter, softened
¾ cup packed brown sugar
¼ cup granulated sugar
1 package (3.4 ounces) butterscotch-flavored instant pudding mix
2 large eggs, slightly beaten
1 teaspoon vanilla extract
1⅓ cups (about 8 ounces) NESTLÉ TOLL HOUSE Butterscotch Flavored Morsels

Nougat Filling
¼ cup (½ stick) butter
1 cup granulated sugar
¼ cup NESTLÉ CARNATION Evaporated Milk
1 jar (7 ounces) marshmallow creme
¼ cup creamy peanut butter
1 teaspoon vanilla extract
1½ cups (about 8 ounces) coarsely chopped salted peanuts

Caramel Layer
1 package (14 ounces) caramels, unwrapped
¼ cup heavy whipping cream

Icing
1 cup (6 ounces) NESTLÉ TOLL HOUSE Milk Chocolate Morsels
⅓ cup NESTLÉ TOLL HOUSE Butterscotch Flavored Morsels
¼ cup creamy peanut butter

For Cookie Base
PREHEAT oven to 350°F. Line 17 × 11 × 1-inch baking pan with parchment paper.

COMBINE flour, baking soda and salt in small bowl. Beat butter, brown sugar and granulated sugar in large mixer bowl until creamy. Add pudding mix, eggs and vanilla extract; mix well. Gradually beat in flour mixture. Stir in 1⅓ cups butterscotch morsels. Spread and pat dough evenly into prepared baking pan.

BAKE for 10 to 11 minutes or until light golden brown. Carefully hold pan 2 to 3 inches above a heat-resistant surface and allow pan to drop. (This creates a chewier cookie base.) Cool completely in pan on wire rack.

continued on page 144

Nutty Nougat Caramel Bites, continued

For Nougat Filling

MELT butter in medium, *heavy-duty* saucepan over medium heat. Add granulated sugar and evaporated milk; stir. Bring to a boil, stirring constantly. Boil, stirring constantly, for 5 minutes. Remove from heat.

STIR in marshmallow creme, peanut butter and vanilla extract. Add peanuts; stir well. Spread nougat mixture over cookie base. Refrigerate for 15 minutes or until set.

For Caramel Layer

COMBINE caramels and whipping cream in medium, *heavy-duty* saucepan. Cook over low heat, stirring constantly, until caramels are melted and mixture is smooth. Spread caramel mixture over nougat layer. Refrigerate for 15 minutes or until set.

For Icing

MELT milk chocolate morsels, ⅓ cup butterscotch morsels and peanut butter in medium, microwave-safe bowl on MEDIUM-HIGH (70%) power for 1 minute; stir. Microwave at additional 10- to 20-second intervals, stirring until smooth. Spread icing over caramel layer. Refrigerate for at least 1 hour.

TO SERVE: Let stand at room temperature for 5 to 10 minutes. Cut into 1-inch pieces. Store in airtight container in refrigerator. *Makes about 15 dozen pieces*

Rocky Road Clusters

2 cups (12-ounce package) NESTLÉ TOLL HOUSE Semi-Sweet
  Chocolate Morsels
1 can (14 ounces) NESTLÉ CARNATION Sweetened Condensed Milk
2½ cups miniature marshmallows
1 cup coarsely chopped nuts
1 teaspoon vanilla extract

LINE baking sheets with wax paper.

COMBINE morsels and sweetened condensed milk in large, microwave-safe bowl. Microwave on HIGH (100%) power for 1 minute; stir. Microwave at additional 10- to 20-second intervals, stirring until smooth. Stir in marshmallows, nuts and vanilla extract.

DROP by heaping tablespoon in mounds onto prepared baking sheets. Refrigerate until firm. *Makes about 2 dozen candies*

Chocolate Peppermint Wafers

3 bars (6-ounce box) NESTLÉ TOLL HOUSE Premier White Baking Bars, broken
     into pieces
12 (about ⅓ cup) coarsely crushed unwrapped hard peppermint candies
1 cup (6 ounces) NESTLÉ TOLL HOUSE Semi-Sweet Chocolate Morsels
1 tablespoon vegetable shortening

LINE 8-inch-square baking pan with foil.

MICROWAVE baking bars in medium, microwave-safe bowl on MEDIUM-HIGH
(70%) power for 1 minute; stir. Microwave at additional 10- to 20-second intervals,
stirring until smooth. Stir in candy. Thinly spread into prepared baking pan.
Refrigerate for 10 minutes or until firm.

REMOVE foil from candy; break into bite-size pieces.

LINE baking sheets with wax paper.

MICROWAVE morsels and vegetable shortening in small, microwave-safe bowl on
HIGH (100%) power for 1 minute; stir. Microwave at additional 10- to 20-second
intervals, stirring until smooth.

DIP candy pieces ¾ of the way into melted chocolate; shake off excess. Place on
prepared baking sheets. Refrigerate until ready to serve.

Makes about 3 dozen candies

Note: To crush candies, place in *heavy-duty* resealable plastic food storage bag; close.
Crush with rolling pin or mallet.

Dazzling Desserts

Quick Tiramisu

1 package (18 ounces) NESTLÉ TOLL HOUSE Refrigerated Sugar Cookie Bar Dough
1 package (8 ounces) ⅓ less fat cream cheese
½ cup granulated sugar
¾ teaspoon TASTER'S CHOICE 100% Pure Instant Coffee dissolved in ¾ cup cold water, *divided*
1 container (8 ounces) frozen nondairy whipped topping, thawed
1 tablespoon NESTLÉ TOLL HOUSE Baking Cocoa

PREHEAT oven to 325°F.

DIVIDE cookie dough into 20 pieces. Shape into 2½ × 1-inch oblong shapes. Place on ungreased baking sheets.

BAKE for 10 to 12 minutes or until light golden brown around edges. Cool on baking sheets for 1 minute; remove to wire racks to cool completely.

BEAT cream cheese and sugar in large mixer bowl until smooth. Beat in ¼ *cup* Taster's Choice. Fold in whipped topping. Layer 6 cookies in 8-inch-square baking dish. Sprinkle each cookie with *1 teaspoon* Taster's Choice. Spread *one-third* cream cheese mixture over cookies. Repeat layers 2 more times with *12* cookies, *remaining* coffee and *remaining* cream cheese mixture. Cover; refrigerate for 2 to 3 hours. Crumble *remaining* cookies over top. Sift cocoa over cookies. Cut into squares. *Makes 6 to 8 servings*

Mom's Special Occasion Ice-Cream Cookie Dessert

Cookies
> 1 package (18 ounces) NESTLÉ TOLL HOUSE Refrigerated Chocolate Chip Cookie Bar Dough

Walnut Mix
> 1 cup chopped walnuts
> 1½ tablespoons butter or margarine, melted
> 1 tablespoon packed brown sugar

Chocolate Sauce
> 1 can (12 fluid ounces) NESTLÉ CARNATION Evaporated Milk
> 1 cup (6 ounces) NESTLÉ TOLL HOUSE Semi-Sweet Chocolate Morsels
> 1 cup powdered sugar
> 1 bar (2 ounces *total*) NESTLÉ TOLL HOUSE Unsweetened Chocolate Baking Bars, broken into pieces
> 2 tablespoons butter or margarine
> 1 tablespoon vanilla extract

> Half gallon vanilla ice cream, softened

For Cookies

BAKE cookies according to package directions; remove to wire racks to cool completely. Chop cooled cookies into small pieces.

For Walnut Mix

PREHEAT oven to 375°F. Grease 8-inch-square baking pan.

COMBINE walnuts, butter and brown sugar in small bowl. Pour into prepared pan. Bake for 8 to 10 minutes; stir well. Cool completely in pan on wire rack.

For Chocolate Sauce

COMBINE evaporated milk, morsels, powdered sugar, baking bar and butter in medium, *heavy-duty* saucepan. Cook over medium-low heat, stirring occasionally, until chocolate is melted. Reduce heat to low; continue cooking, stirring occasionally, for 5 to 7 minutes or until thickened. Remove from heat. Stir in vanilla extract. Cool completely.

continued on page 150

Mom's Special Occasion Ice-Cream Cookie Dessert, continued

To Assemble

WRAP *outside* of 9- or 10-inch springform pan with foil. Spread ⅓ of chopped cookies on bottom of pan. Top with *half* of ice cream and *half* of chocolate sauce. Combine *remaining* chopped cookies and walnut mixture in medium bowl. Spread *half* of cookie-walnut mixture over chocolate sauce. Top with *remaining* ice cream, chocolate sauce (reserving 2 tablespoons) and cookie-walnut mixture.

PLACE *remaining* 2 tablespoons chocolate sauce in small, *heavy-duty* resealable plastic food storage bag. Cut a hole in corner of bag; squeeze to drizzle chocolate sauce over top of dessert. Freeze for at least 4 hours or overnight.

TO SERVE: Let stand at room temperature for 20 minutes. Remove side of springform pan. Cut into slices.

Makes 16 servings

Vanilla Flan

¾ **cup granulated sugar**
 1 **can (12 fluid ounces) NESTLÉ CARNATION Evaporated Milk**
 1 **can (14 ounces) NESTLÉ CARNATION Sweetened Condensed Milk**
 3 **large eggs**
 1 **tablespoon vanilla extract**

PREHEAT oven to 325°F.

HEAT sugar in small, *heavy-duty* saucepan over medium-low heat, stirring constantly, for 3 to 4 minutes or until dissolved and caramel colored. Quickly pour onto bottom of deep-dish 9-inch pie plate; swirl around bottom and side to coat.

COMBINE evaporated milk, sweetened condensed milk, eggs and vanilla extract in medium bowl. Pour into prepared pie plate. Place pie plate in large roasting pan; fill roasting pan with warm water to about 1-inch depth.

BAKE for 45 to 50 minutes or until knife inserted near center comes out clean. Remove flan from water. Cool on wire rack. Refrigerate for 4 hours or overnight.

TO SERVE: Run small spatula around edge of pie plate. Invert serving plate over pie plate. Turn over; shake gently to release. Caramelized sugar forms sauce.

Makes 8 servings

Chocolate Hazelnut Terrine with Raspberry Sauce

Dark Chocolate Layer

    2 cups (12-ounce package) NESTLÉ TOLL HOUSE Semi-Sweet
      Chocolate Morsels
    ⅓ cup butter, cut into pieces
    ¼ cup hazelnut liqueur
    1½ cups heavy whipping cream

Milk Chocolate Layer

    1¾ cups (11.5-ounce package) NESTLÉ TOLL HOUSE Milk Chocolate Morsels
    ⅓ cup butter, cut into pieces

Raspberry Sauce

    1 package (10 ounces) frozen raspberries in syrup, thawed, puréed and strained
    ½ cup water
    1 tablespoon cornstarch
    1 teaspoon granulated sugar

LINE 9 × 5-inch loaf pan with plastic wrap.

For Dark Chocolate Layer

MICROWAVE semi-sweet morsels and ⅓ cup butter in medium, microwave-safe bowl on HIGH (100%) power for 1 minute; stir. Microwave at additional 10- to 20-second intervals, stirring until smooth. Stir in liqueur; cool to room temperature.

WHIP cream in small mixer bowl until stiff peaks form. Fold *2 cups* whipped cream into chocolate mixture. Spoon into prepared loaf pan. Refrigerate *remaining* whipped cream.

For Milk Chocolate Layer

MICROWAVE milk chocolate morsels and ⅓ cup butter in medium, microwave-safe bowl on MEDIUM-HIGH (70%) power for 1 minute; stir. Microwave at additional 10- to 20-second intervals, stirring until smooth. Cool to room temperature. Stir *remaining* whipped cream into chocolate mixture. Spread over dark chocolate layer. Cover; refrigerate for at least 2 hours or until firm.

For Raspberry Sauce

COOK raspberry purée, water, cornstarch and sugar over medium heat, stirring constantly, until mixture comes to a boil; boil for 1 minute. Cover; refrigerate.

TO SERVE: Invert terrine onto serving platter; remove plastic wrap. Cut into ½-inch-thick slices; serve in pool of Raspberry Sauce. *Makes 16 servings*

Rich Chocolate Mousse

1 cup (6 ounces) NESTLÉ TOLL HOUSE Semi-Sweet Chocolate Morsels
3 tablespoons butter, cut into pieces
2 teaspoons TASTER'S CHOICE 100% Pure Instant Coffee
1 tablespoon hot water
2 teaspoons vanilla extract
½ cup heavy whipping cream

MICROWAVE morsels and butter in medium, microwave-safe bowl on HIGH (100%) power for 1 minute; stir. Microwave at additional 10- to 20-second intervals, stirring until smooth. Dissolve Taster's Choice in hot water; stir into chocolate. Stir in vanilla extract; cool to room temperature.

WHIP cream in small mixer bowl on high speed until stiff peaks form; fold into chocolate mixture. Spoon into tall glasses; refrigerate for 1 hour or until set. Garnish as desired.

Makes 2 servings

tip

For best results when beating heavy whipping cream, chill the cream, bowl and beaters first—the cold keeps the fat in the cream solid, thus increasing the volume. The cold also makes the cream whip up faster.

Fruit-Filled Chocolate Chip Meringue Nests

Meringues
    4 large egg whites
    ½ teaspoon salt
    ½ teaspoon cream of tartar
    1 cup granulated sugar
    2 cups (12-ounce package) NESTLÉ TOLL HOUSE Semi-Sweet Chocolate
        Morsels

Chocolate Sauce
    ⅔ cup (5 fluid-ounce can) NESTLÉ CARNATION Evaporated Milk
    1 cup (6 ounces) NESTLÉ TOLL HOUSE Semi-Sweet Chocolate Morsels
    1 tablespoon granulated sugar
    1 teaspoon vanilla extract
        Pinch salt
    3 cups fresh fruit or berries (whole blackberries, blueberries or raspberries,
        sliced kiwi, peaches or strawberries)

For Meringues
PREHEAT oven to 300°F. Lightly grease baking sheets.

BEAT egg whites, salt and cream of tartar in large mixer bowl until soft peaks form. Gradually add sugar; beat until sugar is dissolved. Gently fold in morsels. Spread meringue into ten 3-inch nests with deep wells about 2 inches apart on prepared baking sheets.

BAKE for 35 to 45 minutes or until meringues are dry and crisp. Cool on baking sheets for 5 minutes; remove to wire racks to cool completely.

For Chocolate Sauce
HEAT evaporated milk to a boil in small, *heavy-duty* saucepan. Stir in morsels. Cook, stirring constantly, until mixture is slightly thickened and smooth. Remove from heat; stir in sugar, vanilla extract and salt.

FILL meringues with fruit and drizzle with Chocolate Sauce; serve immediately.

Makes 10 servings

Summer Berry Brownie Torte

Brownie
- ¾ cup granulated sugar
- 6 tablespoons butter or margarine
- 1 tablespoon water
- 1½ cups (9 ounces) NESTLÉ TOLL HOUSE Semi-Sweet Chocolate Morsels, *divided*
- ½ teaspoon vanilla extract
- 2 large eggs
- ⅔ cup all-purpose flour
- ¼ teaspoon baking soda
- ¼ teaspoon salt

Filling
- ½ cup heavy whipping cream
- ¼ cup granulated sugar

- 2 cups sliced strawberries or other fresh berries

For Brownie
PREHEAT oven to 350°F. Grease and wax paper-line 9-inch-round cake pan.

COMBINE sugar, butter and water in small, *heavy-duty* saucepan. Bring to a boil, stirring constantly; remove from heat. Add *¾ cup* morsels; stir until smooth. Stir in vanilla extract. Add eggs, one at a time, stirring well after each addition. Add flour, baking soda and salt; stir until well blended. Stir in *¾ cup* morsels. Pour into prepared cake pan.

BAKE for 20 to 25 minutes or until wooden pick inserted in center comes out slightly sticky. Cool for 15 minutes in pan. Invert onto wire rack; remove wax paper. Turn right side up; cool completely.

For Filling
BEAT cream and sugar in small mixer bowl until stiff peaks form.

To Assemble
SPREAD filling over brownie; top with berries.

Makes 10 to 12 servings

Individual Chocolate Espresso Soufflés

    Nonstick cooking spray
 2 tablespoons granulated sugar
½ cup NESTLÉ TOLL HOUSE Baking Cocoa
½ cup hot water
 3 tablespoons French Roast NESCAFÉ Gourmet Instant Coffee
 2 tablespoons butter
 3 tablespoons all-purpose flour
¾ cup NESTLÉ CARNATION Evaporated Fat Free Milk
¾ cup granulated sugar, *divided*
 4 large egg whites
    Pinch of salt
    Powdered sugar

PREHEAT oven to 375°F. Spray eight 6-ounce custard cups with nonstick cooking spray; sprinkle evenly with 2 tablespoons granulated sugar.

COMBINE cocoa, water and Nescafé in medium bowl; stir until smooth. Melt butter in small saucepan over medium heat. Stir in flour; cook, stirring constantly, for 1 minute. Stir in evaporated milk and ½ *cup* granulated sugar. Cook, whisking frequently, for 2 to 3 minutes or until mixture is slightly thickened. Remove from heat. Add to cocoa mixture; stir until smooth.

BEAT egg whites and a pinch of salt in small mixer bowl until soft peaks form. Gradually beat in *remaining* granulated sugar until stiff peaks form. Fold *one-fourth* of egg whites into chocolate mixture to lighten. Fold in *remaining* egg whites gently but thoroughly. Pour mixture into prepared cups, filling ¾ full. Place on baking sheet.

BAKE for 18 to 20 minutes or until wooden pick inserted in center comes out moist but not wet. Sprinkle with powdered sugar. Serve immediately.   *Makes 8 servings*

Holiday Bread Pudding

16 slices bread, cubed
1 cup dried cranberries or raisins
2 cans (12 fluid ounces *each*) NESTLÉ CARNATION Evaporated Milk
4 large eggs, lightly beaten
4 tablespoons butter, melted
¾ cup packed brown sugar
1 tablespoon vanilla extract
1 teaspoon ground cinnamon
½ teaspoon ground nutmeg
   Caramel sauce (optional)

PREHEAT oven to 350°F. Grease 12 × 8-inch baking dish.

COMBINE bread and cranberries in large bowl. Combine evaporated milk, eggs, butter, sugar, vanilla extract, cinnamon and nutmeg in medium bowl. Pour egg mixture over bread mixture; combine well. Pour mixture into prepared baking dish. Let stand for 10 minutes.

BAKE for 35 to 45 minutes or until knife inserted in center comes out clean. Top with caramel sauce. Garnish as desired. *Makes 8 servings*

tip

To melt 4 tablespoons of butter quickly and easily, place it in a microwave-safe dish and cover with plastic wrap. Microwave on HIGH (100%) power for 50 to 60 seconds.

Chocolate Rhapsody

Cake Layer
- ⅔ cup all-purpose flour
- ½ teaspoon baking powder
- ¼ teaspoon salt
- 6 tablespoons butter or margarine, softened
- ½ cup granulated sugar
- 1 large egg
- 1 teaspoon vanilla extract
- ¼ cup milk

Chocolate Layer
- 2 cups (12-ounce package) NESTLÉ TOLL HOUSE Semi-Sweet Chocolate Morsels
- ¾ cup heavy whipping cream

Raspberry Mousse Layer
- ⅓ cup granulated sugar
- 2 tablespoons water
- 1 teaspoon cornstarch
- 2 cups (8 ounces) slightly sweetened or unsweetened frozen raspberries, *thawed*
- 3 bars (6-ounce box) NESTLÉ TOLL HOUSE Premier White Baking Bars, broken into pieces
- 1¾ cups heavy whipping cream, *divided*
- 1 teaspoon vanilla extract
- Sweetened whipped cream (optional)
- Fresh raspberries (optional)

For Cake Layer

PREHEAT oven to 350°F. Grease 9-inch springform pan.

COMBINE flour, baking powder and salt in small bowl. Beat butter and sugar in small mixer bowl until creamy. Beat in egg and vanilla extract. Alternately beat in flour mixture and milk. Spread into prepared springform pan.

BAKE for 15 to 20 minutes or until lightly browned. Cool completely in pan on wire rack.

For Chocolate Layer

MICROWAVE morsels and cream in medium, microwave-safe bowl on HIGH (100%) power for 1 minute; stir. Microwave at additional 10- to 20-second intervals, stirring until smooth. Cool completely.

continued on page 162

Chocolate Rhapsody, continued

For Raspberry Mousse Layer

COMBINE sugar, water and cornstarch in medium saucepan; stir in raspberries. Bring mixture to a boil. Boil, stirring constantly, for 1 minute. Cool completely.

MICROWAVE baking bars and ½ *cup* cream in medium, microwave-safe bowl on MEDIUM-HIGH (70%) power for 1 minute; stir. Microwave at additional 10- to 20-second intervals, stirring until smooth. Cool completely. Stir into raspberry mixture.

BEAT *remaining* cream and vanilla extract in large mixer bowl until stiff peaks form. Fold raspberry mixture into whipped cream.

To Assemble

REMOVE side of springform pan; dust off crumbs from cake. Grease inside of pan; reattach side. Spread ½ *cup* chocolate mixture over cake layer; freeze for 5 minutes. Spoon raspberry mousse over chocolate; freeze for 10 minutes. Carefully spread *remaining* chocolate mixture over raspberry mousse. Refrigerate for at least 4 hours or until firm. Carefully remove side of springform pan. Garnish with whipped cream and raspberries.

Makes 12 servings

Fruit Medley Dessert

1 package (18 ounces) NESTLÉ TOLL HOUSE Refrigerated Sugar Cookie Bar Dough
1 container (32 ounces) lowfat vanilla yogurt or 1 quart vanilla frozen yogurt
4 cups fresh fruit (blueberries, raspberries, sliced apples, cherries, nectarines, peaches and/or strawberries)

PREHEAT oven to 325°F.

ROLL chilled dough on floured surface to ¼-inch thickness. Cut out 24 shapes using 3-inch cookie cutters. Place on ungreased baking sheets.

BAKE for 10 to 14 minutes or until edges are light golden brown. Cool on baking sheets for 2 minutes; remove to wire racks to cool completely.

PLACE two cookies on each plate. Top with ½ cup yogurt and ½ cup fruit mixture. Place third cookie on top.

Makes 8 servings

Dipped Fruit

2 cups (12-ounce package) NESTLÉ TOLL HOUSE Semi-Sweet Chocolate
   Morsels or NESTLÉ TOLL HOUSE Premier White Morsels
2 tablespoons vegetable shortening
24 bite-size pieces fresh fruit (strawberries, orange, kiwi, banana or melon),
   rinsed and patted dry

LINE baking sheet with wax paper.

MICROWAVE morsels and shortening in medium, microwave-safe bowl on
MEDIUM-HIGH (70%) power for 1 minute; stir. Microwave at additional
10- to 20-second intervals, stirring until smooth.

DIP fruit into melted morsels; shake off excess. Place on prepared baking sheet;
refrigerate until set.   *Makes about 2 dozen pieces*

For a fancy drizzle
MICROWAVE ½ cup NESTLÉ TOLL HOUSE Semi-Sweet Chocolate or Premier
White Morsels or Baking Bars, broken in pieces, in small, *heavy-duty* resealable plastic
food storage bag on MEDIUM-HIGH (70%) power for 1 minute; knead. Microwave
at additional 10- to 20-second intervals, kneading until smooth. Cut tiny corner from
bag; squeeze to drizzle over fruit. Refrigerate until set.

Baked Custard

4 large eggs
½ cup granulated sugar
½ teaspoon salt
1 can (12 fluid ounces) NESTLÉ CARNATION Evaporated Milk
1 cup water
1 teaspoon vanilla extract
   Ground nutmeg

PREHEAT oven to 350°F.

COMBINE eggs, sugar and salt in large mixer bowl. Add evaporated milk, water and
vanilla extract; beat until mixed. Pour into six 6-ounce custard cups. Sprinkle with
nutmeg. Place cups in 13 × 9-inch baking pan; fill pan with hot water to 1-inch depth.

BAKE for 35 to 40 minutes or until knife inserted near center comes out clean.
Remove cups to wire rack to cool completely. Refrigerate until ready to serve.

Makes 6 servings

Breakfast & Brunch

Stuffed French Toast with Fresh Berry Topping

2 cups mixed fresh berries (strawberries, raspberries, blueberries and/or blackberries)

2 tablespoons granulated sugar

⅔ cup lowfat ricotta cheese

¼ cup strawberry preserves

3 large eggs

⅔ cup NESTLÉ CARNATION Evaporated Fat Free Milk

2 tablespoons packed brown sugar

2 teaspoons vanilla extract

12 slices (about ¾-inch thick) French bread

Vegetable oil, butter or margarine

Powdered sugar (optional)

Maple syrup, heated (optional)

COMBINE berries and granulated sugar in small bowl. Combine ricotta cheese and strawberry preserves in small bowl; mix well. Combine eggs, evaporated milk, brown sugar and vanilla extract in pie plate or shallow bowl; mix well.

SPREAD ricotta-preserve mixture evenly over *6 slices* of bread. Top with *remaining* slices of bread to form sandwiches.

HEAT small amount of vegetable oil in large, nonstick skillet or griddle over medium heat. Dip sandwiches in egg mixture, coating both sides. Cook on each side for about 2 minutes or until golden brown.

SPRINKLE with powdered sugar; top with berries. Serve with maple syrup.

Makes 6 servings

Pumpkin Cranberry Bread

3 cups all-purpose flour

1 tablespoon plus 2 teaspoons pumpkin pie spice

2 teaspoons baking soda

1½ teaspoons salt

3 cups granulated sugar

1 can (15 ounces) LIBBY'S 100% Pure Pumpkin

4 large eggs

1 cup vegetable oil

½ cup orange juice or water

1 cup sweetened dried, fresh or frozen cranberries

PREHEAT oven to 350°F. Grease and flour two 9 × 5-inch loaf pans.

COMBINE flour, pumpkin pie spice, baking soda and salt in large bowl. Combine sugar, pumpkin, eggs, vegetable oil and orange juice in large mixer bowl; beat until just blended. Add pumpkin mixture to flour mixture; stir just until moistened. Fold in cranberries. Spoon batter into prepared loaf pans.

BAKE for 60 to 65 minutes or until wooden pick inserted in center comes out clean. Cool in pans on wire racks for 10 minutes; remove to wire racks to cool completely.

Makes 2 loaves

For Three 8 × 4-inch Loaf Pans
PREPARE as above. Bake for 55 to 60 minutes.

For Five or Six 5 × 3-inch Mini-Loaf Pans
PREPARE as above. Bake for 50 to 55 minutes.

Chocolate Streusel Pecan Muffins

Topping

¼ cup all-purpose flour

¼ cup packed brown sugar

¼ teaspoon ground cinnamon

2 tablespoons butter, melted

¼ cup chopped pecans

Muffins

1¾ cups (11.5-ounce package) NESTLÉ TOLL HOUSE Milk Chocolate Morsels, *divided*

⅓ cup milk

3 tablespoons butter

1 cup all-purpose flour

2 tablespoons granulated sugar

2 teaspoons baking powder

¼ teaspoon ground cinnamon

¾ cup chopped pecans

1 large egg

½ teaspoon vanilla extract

For Topping

COMBINE flour, brown sugar, cinnamon and butter in small bowl with fork until mixture resembles coarse crumbs. Stir in nuts.

For Muffins

PREHEAT oven to 375°F. Grease or paper-line 12 muffin cups.

COMBINE *1 cup* morsels, milk and butter in top of double boiler over hot (not boiling) water. Stir until morsels are melted and mixture is smooth.

COMBINE flour, granulated sugar, baking powder, cinnamon, pecans and *remaining* morsels in large bowl.

COMBINE egg, vanilla extract and melted morsel mixture in small bowl; stir into flour mixture just until moistened. Spoon into prepared muffin cups, filling ⅔ full. Sprinkle with topping.

BAKE for 20 to 25 minutes. Cool in pan for 5 minutes; remove to wire rack to cool completely.

Makes 12 muffins

Butterscotch Sticky Buns

3 tablespoons butter or margarine, *divided*
2 packages (8 ounces *each*) refrigerated crescent dinner rolls
1⅔ cups (11-ounce package) NESTLÉ TOLL HOUSE Butterscotch Flavored Morsels, *divided*
½ cup chopped pecans
¼ cup granulated sugar
1½ teaspoons lemon juice
1½ teaspoons water
1 teaspoon ground cinnamon

PREHEAT oven to 375°F.

PLACE *1 tablespoon* butter in 13 × 9-inch baking pan; melt in oven for 2 to 4 minutes or until butter sizzles. Unroll dinner rolls; separate into 16 triangles. Sprinkle triangles with *1⅓ cups* morsels. Starting at shortest side, roll up each triangle; arrange in prepared baking pan.

BAKE for 15 to 20 minutes or until lightly browned.

MICROWAVE *remaining* morsels and *remaining* butter in medium, microwave-safe bowl on MEDIUM-HIGH (70%) power for 30 seconds; stir. Microwave at additional 10- to 20-second intervals, stirring until smooth. Stir in nuts, sugar, lemon juice, water and cinnamon. Pour over hot rolls.

BAKE for 5 minutes or until bubbly. Immediately loosen buns from pan. Cool in pan on wire rack for 10 minutes; serve warm. *Makes 16 buns*

Donna's Heavenly Orange Chip Scones

4 cups all-purpose flour
1 cup granulated sugar
4 teaspoons baking powder
½ teaspoon baking soda
½ teaspoon salt
1 cup (6 ounces) NESTLÉ TOLL HOUSE Semi-Sweet Chocolate Mini Morsels
1 cup golden raisins
1 tablespoon grated orange peel
1 cup (2 sticks) unsalted butter, cut into pieces and softened
1 cup buttermilk
3 large eggs, *divided*
1 teaspoon orange extract
1 tablespoon milk
Icing (recipe follows)

PREHEAT oven to 350°F. Lightly grease baking sheets.

COMBINE flour, granulated sugar, baking powder, baking soda and salt in large bowl. Add morsels, raisins and orange peel; mix well. Cut in butter with pastry blender or two knives until mixture resembles coarse crumbs. Combine buttermilk, *2 eggs* and orange extract in small bowl. Pour buttermilk mixture into flour mixture; mix just until a sticky dough is formed. Do not overmix. Drop by ¼ cupfuls onto prepared baking sheets. Combine *remaining* egg and milk in small bowl. Brush egg mixture over top of dough.

BAKE for 18 to 22 minutes or until wooden pick inserted in center comes out clean. For best results, bake one baking sheet at a time. Cool on wire racks for 10 minutes. Drizzle scones with icing. Serve warm. *Makes 2 dozen scones*

Icing
COMBINE 2 cups powdered sugar, ¼ cup orange juice, 1 tablespoon grated orange peel and 1 teaspoon orange extract in medium bowl. Mix until smooth.

Hash Brown Casserole

3 cartons (4 ounces *each*) cholesterol-free egg product or 6 large eggs, well beaten
1 can (12 fluid ounces) NESTLÉ CARNATION Evaporated Milk
1 teaspoon salt
½ teaspoon ground black pepper
1 package (30 ounces) frozen shredded hash brown potatoes
2 cups (8 ounces) shredded cheddar cheese
1 medium onion, chopped
1 small green bell pepper, chopped
1 cup diced ham (optional)

PREHEAT oven to 350°F. Grease 13 × 9-inch baking dish.

COMBINE egg product, evaporated milk, salt and black pepper in large bowl. Add potatoes, cheese, onion, bell pepper and ham; mix well. Pour mixture into prepared baking dish.

BAKE for 60 to 65 minutes or until set.   *Makes 12 servings*

Note: For a lower fat version of this recipe, use cholesterol-free egg product, substitute NESTLÉ CARNATION Evaporated Fat Free Milk for Evaporated Milk and 10 slices turkey bacon, cooked and chopped, for the diced ham. Proceed as above.

Mini Pumpkin Muffin Mix

3 cups all-purpose flour
1 cup granulated sugar
1 cup raisins, sweetened dried cranberries or chopped nuts (optional)
4 teaspoons baking powder
1½ teaspoons salt
1 teaspoon ground cinnamon
1 teaspoon ground nutmeg
1 can (15 ounces) LIBBY'S 100% Pure Pumpkin

COMBINE all ingredients, except pumpkin, in large bowl. Pour into 1-quart resealable plastic food storage bag; seal. Wrap muffin mix and can of pumpkin in fabric; tie with ribbon or twine.

Recipe to Attach

Pour muffin mix into large bowl. Cut in ½ cup vegetable shortening with pastry blender until mixture is fine. Add 1 cup LIBBY'S 100% Pure Pumpkin, 1 cup milk and 2 large eggs; mix until just moistened. Spoon into greased or paper-lined mini-muffin pans, filling ⅔ full. Bake in preheated 400°F. oven for 15 to 20 minutes. Cool in pans for 5 minutes; remove to wire racks. Sprinkle with powdered sugar, if desired. Makes about 60 mini muffins.

Down-Home Sausage Gravy

1 package (16 ounces) fresh breakfast sausage
2 tablespoons finely chopped onion
6 tablespoons all-purpose flour
2 cans (12 fluid ounces *each*) NESTLÉ CARNATION Evaporated Milk
1 cup water
¼ teaspoon salt
Hot pepper sauce to taste
Hot biscuits

COMBINE sausage and onion in large skillet. Cook over medium-low heat, stirring occasionally, until sausage is no longer pink. Stir in flour; mix well. Stir in evaporated milk, water, salt and hot pepper sauce. Cook, stirring occasionally, until mixture comes to a boil. Cook for 1 to 2 minutes.

SERVE immediately over biscuits.   *Makes 8 to 10 servings*

Chocolate Brunch Waffles

2¼ cups all-purpose flour
½ cup granulated sugar
1 tablespoon baking powder
¾ teaspoon salt
1 cup (6 ounces) NESTLÉ TOLL HOUSE Semi-Sweet Chocolate Morsels
¾ cup (1½ sticks) butter or margarine
1½ cups milk
3 large eggs, lightly beaten
1 tablespoon vanilla extract
Toppings (whipped cream, chocolate shavings, sifted powdered sugar, fresh fruit, ice cream)

COMBINE flour, sugar, baking powder and salt in large bowl. Microwave morsels and butter in medium, microwave-safe bowl on HIGH (100%) power for 1 minute; stir. Microwave at additional 10- to 20-second intervals, stirring until smooth. Cool to room temperature. Stir in milk, eggs and vanilla extract. Add chocolate mixture to flour mixture; stir (batter will be thick).

COOK in Belgian waffle maker* according to manufacturer's directions. Serve warm with your choice of toppings. *Makes 10 Belgian waffle squares*

Can also be cooked in standard waffle maker (makes about 20 standard-size waffle squares).

Toll House® Crumbcake

Topping

⅓ cup packed brown sugar

1 tablespoon all-purpose flour

2 tablespoons butter or margarine, softened

½ cup chopped nuts

2 cups (12-ounce package) NESTLÉ TOLL HOUSE Semi-Sweet Chocolate Mini Morsels, *divided*

Cake

1¾ cups all-purpose flour

1 teaspoon baking powder

1 teaspoon baking soda

¼ teaspoon salt

¾ cup granulated sugar

½ cup (1 stick) butter or margarine, softened

1 teaspoon vanilla extract

3 large eggs

1 cup sour cream

PREHEAT oven to 350°F. Grease 13 × 9-inch baking pan.

For Topping

COMBINE brown sugar, flour and butter in small bowl with pastry blender or two knives until crumbly. Stir in nuts and *½ cup* morsels.

For Cake

COMBINE flour, baking powder, baking soda and salt in small bowl. Beat granulated sugar, butter and vanilla extract in large mixer bowl until creamy. Add eggs, one at a time, beating well after each addition. Gradually add flour mixture alternately with sour cream. Fold in *remaining* morsels. Spread into prepared baking pan; sprinkle with topping.

BAKE for 25 to 35 minutes or until wooden pick inserted in center comes out clean. Cool in pan on wire rack.   *Makes 12 servings*

Blueberry White Chip Muffins

    2 cups all-purpose flour
 ½ cup granulated sugar
 ¼ cup packed brown sugar
2½ teaspoons baking powder
 ½ teaspoon salt
 ¾ cup milk
    1 large egg, lightly beaten
 ¼ cup butter or margarine, melted
 ½ teaspoon grated lemon peel
    2 cups (12-ounce package) NESTLÉ TOLL HOUSE Premier White Morsels,
         divided
1½ cups fresh or frozen blueberries
     Streusel Topping (recipe follows)

PREHEAT oven to 375°F. Paper-line 18 muffin cups.

COMBINE flour, granulated sugar, brown sugar, baking powder and salt in large bowl. Stir in milk, egg, butter and lemon peel. Stir in *1½ cups* morsels and blueberries. Spoon into prepared muffin cups, filling almost full. Sprinkle with Streusel Topping.

BAKE for 22 to 25 minutes or until wooden pick inserted in center comes out clean. Cool in pans for 5 minutes; remove to wire racks to cool slightly.

PLACE *remaining* morsels in small, *heavy-duty* resealable plastic food storage bag. Microwave on MEDIUM-HIGH (70%) power for 30 seconds; knead. Microwave at additional 10- to 20-second intervals, kneading until smooth. Cut tiny corner from bag; squeeze to drizzle over muffins. Serve warm.   *Makes 18 muffins*

Streusel Topping
COMBINE ⅓ cup granulated sugar, ¼ cup all-purpose flour and ¼ teaspoon ground cinnamon in small bowl. Cut in 3 tablespoons butter or margarine with pastry blender or two knives until mixture resembles coarse crumbs.

Breakfast Sausage Casserole

1 package (16 ounces) fresh breakfast sausage, cooked, drained and crumbled
4 cups cubed day-old bread
2 cups (8 ounces) shredded sharp cheddar cheese
2 cans (12 fluid ounces *each*) NESTLÉ CARNATION Evaporated Milk
10 large eggs, lightly beaten
1 teaspoon dry mustard
¼ teaspoon onion powder
   Ground black pepper to taste

GREASE 13 × 9-inch baking dish. Place bread in prepared baking dish. Sprinkle with cheese. Combine evaporated milk, eggs, dry mustard, onion powder and pepper in medium bowl. Pour evenly over bread and cheese. Sprinkle with sausage. Cover; refrigerate overnight.

PREHEAT oven to 325°F.

BAKE for 55 to 60 minutes or until cheese is golden brown. Cover with foil if top browns too quickly.   *Makes 10 to 12 servings*

Cream Cheese Chocolate Chip Pastry Cookies

1 package (17.25 ounces) frozen puff pastry sheets, thawed
1 package (8 ounces) cream cheese, softened
3 tablespoons granulated sugar
1¾ cups (11.5-ounce package) NESTLÉ TOLL HOUSE Milk Chocolate Morsels, *divided*

UNFOLD *1* pastry sheet on lightly floured surface. Roll out to make 14 × 10-inch rectangle. Combine cream cheese and sugar in small bowl until smooth. Spread *half* of cream cheese mixture over pastry, leaving 1-inch border on one long side. Sprinkle with *half* of morsels. Roll up pastry starting at long side covered with cream cheese. Seal end by moistening with water. Repeat steps with *remaining* ingredients. Refrigerate for 1 hour.

PREHEAT oven to 375°F. Lightly grease baking sheets or line with parchment paper.

CUT rolls crosswise into 1-inch-thick slices. Place cut side down on prepared baking sheets.

BAKE for 20 to 25 minutes or until golden brown. Cool on baking sheets for 2 minutes; remove to wire racks to cool completely.   *Makes about 2 dozen cookies*

Orange Brunch Muffins

3 cups all-purpose baking mix
¾ cup all-purpose flour
⅔ cup granulated sugar
2 large eggs, lightly beaten
½ cup plain yogurt
½ cup orange juice
1 tablespoon grated orange peel
2 cups (12-ounce package) NESTLÉ TOLL HOUSE Premier White Morsels,
    divided
½ cup chopped macadamia nuts or walnuts

PREHEAT oven to 375°F. Grease or paper-line 18 muffin cups.

COMBINE baking mix, flour and sugar in large bowl. Add eggs, yogurt, orange juice and orange peel; stir just until blended. Stir in *1⅓ cups* morsels. Spoon into prepared muffin cups, filling ¾ full. Sprinkle with nuts.

BAKE for 18 to 22 minutes or until wooden pick inserted in center comes out clean. Cool in pans for 10 minutes; remove to wire racks to cool slightly.

MICROWAVE *remaining* morsels in small, *heavy-duty* resealable plastic food storage bag on MEDIUM-HIGH (70%) power for 1 minute; knead. Microwave at additional 10- to 20-second intervals, kneading until smooth. Cut tiny corner from bag; squeeze to drizzle over muffins. Serve warm.   *Makes 18 muffins*

Toll House® Mini Morsel Pancakes

2½ cups all-purpose flour
1 cup (6 ounces) NESTLÉ TOLL HOUSE Semi-Sweet Chocolate Mini Morsels
1 tablespoon baking powder
½ teaspoon salt
1¾ cups milk
2 large eggs
⅓ cup vegetable oil
⅓ cup packed brown sugar
Powdered sugar
Fresh sliced strawberries
Maple syrup

COMBINE flour, morsels, baking powder and salt in large bowl. Combine milk, eggs, vegetable oil and brown sugar in medium bowl; add to flour mixture. Stir just until moistened (batter may be lumpy).

HEAT griddle or skillet over medium heat; brush lightly with vegetable oil. Pour *¼ cup* of batter onto hot griddle; cook until bubbles begin to burst. Turn; continue to cook for about 1 minute longer or until golden. Repeat with *remaining* batter.

SPRINKLE with powdered sugar; top with strawberries. Serve with maple syrup.

Makes about 18 pancakes

tip

A pancake is ready to turn when the top is bubbly all over and starts to appear dry. Turn the pancake only once and cook until lightly browned on the underside. You can keep pancakes warm by placing them on a warmed plate or baking dish in a 200°F. oven. Layer paper towels between the pancakes to absorb steam and keep them from getting soggy.

Petit Pain au Chocolate

1 package (17.25 ounces) frozen puff pastry sheets, thawed
1 cup (6 ounces) NESTLÉ TOLL HOUSE Milk Chocolate Morsels, *divided*
1 large egg, beaten
1 bar (2 ounces *total*) NESTLÉ TOLL HOUSE Semi-Sweet Chocolate
    Baking Bars, broken into pieces
2 tablespoons butter or margarine
1 cup powdered sugar
2 tablespoons hot water

PREHEAT oven to 350°F. Grease 2 baking sheets.

UNFOLD *1* pastry sheet on lightly floured surface. Roll out to make 10-inch square. Cut into 4 squares. Place *2 tablespoons* morsels in center of each square. Brush edges lightly with beaten egg and fold squares to form triangles. Press edges to seal. Place on prepared baking sheet about 2 inches apart. Repeat with *remaining* pastry sheet. Brush top of each pastry with beaten egg.

BAKE for 15 to 17 minutes or until puffed and golden. Cool on baking sheets for 2 minutes; remove to wire racks to cool completely.

MELT baking bar and butter in small, microwave-safe bowl on HIGH (100%) power for 30 seconds; stir. Microwave at additional 10- to 20-second intervals, stirring until smooth. Stir in sugar. Add water, stirring until icing is smooth, adding additional water, if necessary. Drizzle icing over pastries.   *Makes 8 pastries*

Ham and Swiss Quiche

1 *unbaked* 9-inch (4-cup volume) deep-dish pie shell
1 cup (4 ounces) shredded Swiss cheese, *divided*
1 cup finely chopped cooked ham
2 green onions, sliced
1 can (12 fluid ounces) NESTLÉ CARNATION Evaporated Milk
3 large eggs
¼ cup all-purpose flour
¼ teaspoon salt
⅛ teaspoon ground black pepper

PREHEAT oven to 350°F.

SPRINKLE *½ cup* cheese, ham and green onions into pie crust. Whisk together evaporated milk, eggs, flour, salt and pepper in large bowl. Pour mixture into pie shell; sprinkle with *remaining* cheese.

BAKE for 45 to 50 minutes or until knife inserted near center comes out clean. Cool on wire rack for 10 minutes before serving.   *Makes 8 servings*

For Mini-Quiche Appetizers: Use 1½ packages (3 crusts) refrigerated pie crusts. Grease miniature muffin pans. Unfold crust on lightly floured surface. Cut fourteen 2½-inch circles from each crust. Press 1 circle of dough into bottom and up side of each cup. Repeat with *remaining* crusts. Combine cheese, ham, green onions, ⅔ cup *(5 fluid-ounce can)* evaporated milk, 2 eggs (lightly beaten), *2 tablespoons* flour, salt and pepper in large bowl; mix well. Spoon mixture into crusts, filling ¾ full. Bake in preheated 350°F. oven for 20 to 25 minutes or until crusts are golden brown. Cool slightly; lift quiche from cup with tip of knife. Serve warm or cool and freeze for future entertaining. Makes 3½ dozen.

Pumpkin Streusel Coffeecake

Streusel Topping
- ½ cup all-purpose flour
- ¼ cup packed brown sugar
- 1½ teaspoons ground cinnamon
- 3 tablespoons butter or margarine
- ½ cup coarsely chopped nuts

Coffeecake
- 2 cups all-purpose flour
- 2 teaspoons baking powder
- 1½ teaspoons ground cinnamon
- ½ teaspoon baking soda
- ¼ teaspoon salt
- 1 cup (2 sticks) butter or margarine, softened
- 1 cup granulated sugar
- 2 large eggs
- 1 cup LIBBY'S 100% Pure Pumpkin
- 1 teaspoon vanilla extract

PREHEAT oven to 350°F. Grease and flour 9-inch-round cake pan.

For Streusel Topping
COMBINE flour, brown sugar and cinnamon in medium bowl. Cut in butter with pastry blender or two knives until mixture is crumbly; stir in nuts.

For Coffeecake
COMBINE flour, baking powder, cinnamon, baking soda and salt in small bowl. Beat butter and granulated sugar in large mixer bowl until creamy. Add eggs, one at a time, beating well after each addition. Beat in pumpkin and vanilla extract. Gradually beat in flour mixture.

SPOON *half* of batter into prepared cake pan. Sprinkle *half* of Streusel Topping over batter. Spoon *remaining* batter evenly over Streusel Topping; sprinkle with *remaining* Streusel Topping.

BAKE for 45 to 50 minutes or until wooden pick inserted in center comes out clean. Cool in pan on wire rack for 10 minutes; remove to wire rack to cool completely.

Makes 10 servings

Index

Index

METRIC CONVERSION CHART

VOLUME
MEASUREMENTS (dry)

⅛ teaspoon = 0.5 mL
¼ teaspoon = 1 mL
½ teaspoon = 2 mL
¾ teaspoon = 4 mL
1 teaspoon = 5 mL
1 tablespoon = 15 mL
2 tablespoons = 30 mL
¼ cup = 60 mL
⅓ cup = 75 mL
½ cup = 125 mL
⅔ cup = 150 mL
¾ cup = 175 mL
1 cup = 250 mL
2 cups = 1 pint = 500 mL
3 cups = 750 mL
4 cups = 1 quart = 1 L

VOLUME MEASUREMENTS (fluid)

1 fluid ounce (2 tablespoons) = 30 mL
4 fluid ounces (½ cup) = 125 mL
8 fluid ounces (1 cup) = 250 mL
12 fluid ounces (1½ cups) = 375 mL
16 fluid ounces (2 cups) = 500 mL

WEIGHTS (mass)

½ ounce = 15 g
1 ounce = 30 g
3 ounces = 90 g
4 ounces = 120 g
8 ounces = 225 g
10 ounces = 285 g
12 ounces = 360 g
16 ounces = 1 pound = 450 g

DIMENSIONS

1/16 inch = 2 mm
⅛ inch = 3 mm
¼ inch = 6 mm
½ inch = 1.5 cm
¾ inch = 2 cm
1 inch = 2.5 cm

OVEN
TEMPERATURES

250°F = 120°C
275°F = 140°C
300°F = 150°C
325°F = 160°C
350°F = 180°C
375°F = 190°C
400°F = 200°C
425°F = 220°C
450°F = 230°C

BAKING PAN SIZES

Utensil	Size in Inches/Quarts	Metric Volume	Size in Centimeters
Baking or Cake Pan (square or rectangular)	8×8×2	2 L	20×20×5
	9×9×2	2.5 L	23×23×5
	12×8×2	3 L	30×20×5
	13×9×2	3.5 L	33×23×5
Loaf Pan	8×4×3	1.5 L	20×10×7
	9×5×3	2 L	23×13×7
Round Layer Cake Pan	8×1½	1.2 L	20×4
	9×1½	1.5 L	23×4
Pie Plate	8×1¼	750 mL	20×3
	9×1¼	1 L	23×3
Baking Dish or Casserole	1 quart	1 L	—
	1½ quart	1.5 L	—
	2 quart	2 L	—